KLASSENARBEITEN

AF178623

Englisch 10. Klasse

Heidi Schmitt

STARK

© 2021 Stark Verlag GmbH, St.-Martin-Straße 82, 81541 München
1. Auflage 2013
www.stark-verlag.de

Inhalt

Auf die MP3-Dateien für die Hörverstehensaufgaben kannst du online auf der Plattform MyStark zugreifen.

Autorin: Heidi Schmitt

Sprecher*innen: Kenneth Byrne, Daniel Holzberg, Erika Stoll, Holli Winter

Vorwort

Liebe Schülerin, lieber Schüler,

in diesem Buch findest du zahlreiche Aufgaben-Sets, mit denen du dich auf Tests und Klassenarbeiten im Fach Englisch vorbereiten kannst. Die Klassenarbeiten und Tests orientieren sich an den Lehrplanthemen und die Aufgabenformen sind vielfältig und entsprechen denen, die du aus dem Unterricht kennst. Folgende Hinweise helfen dir bei der Arbeit mit dem Buch:

- Vor den Tests und Klassenarbeiten steht immer eine **Zeitangabe**, die angibt, wie lange du für die Bearbeitung brauchen darfst. Halte dich bitte an die vorgegebenen Zeiten, damit du bei einem Test oder einer Klassenarbeit in der Schule nicht in Zeitnot gerätst.

- Natürlich kannst du auch nur einzelne Aufgaben aus den Tests und Klassenarbeiten bearbeiten. Verkürze deine Arbeitszeit dann entsprechend!

- Damit du die Aufgaben selbstständig bearbeiten kannst, findest du nach jedem mit Punkten versehenen Aufgabenteil entsprechende **Lösungsvorschläge**. Hier stehen auch immer **nützliche Tipps und Hinweise**, die dir bei der Bearbeitung helfen sollen. Probiere jedoch zunächst die Aufgaben selbstständig zu lösen, bevor du dir die Hilfen anschaust.

- Außerdem findest du hier einen **Notenschlüssel**, damit du weißt, welche Note du erzielt hättest.

- Die den Tests und Klassenarbeiten vorangestellte **Kurzgrammatik** steht dir zum schnellen Nachschlagen bei grammatikalischen Schwierigkeiten zur Verfügung.

- Auf die **MP3-Dateien** für die Hörverstehensaufgaben kannst du online auf der Plattform **MyStark** zugreifen. Die Dateien können auch für den Offline-Gebrauch heruntergeladen werden. Auf der vorderen Umschlaginnenseite findest du einen Link und deinen persönlichen Zugangscode.

Wähle die Klassenarbeiten und Tests, die du vor einer Prüfung übst, nicht nur nach dem Thema aus, sondern auch nach den Kompetenzbereichen. In der nächsten Klassenarbeit kommt eine Mediation dran? Dann übe die Mediation! Ihr habt im Unterricht die richtige Verwendung der Zeiten wiederholt? Dann löse die entsprechenden Aufgaben!

Viel Spaß beim Üben und viel Erfolg bei der nächsten Klassenarbeit!

Heidi Schmitt

Kurzgrammatik

Besonderheiten einiger Wortarten

1 Adjektive und Adverbien – *Adjectives and Adverbs*
Bildung und Verwendung von Adverbien – *Formation and Use of Adverbs*

Bildung

Adjektiv + *-ly*

glad   → glad<u>ly</u>

Ausnahmen:
- *-y* am Wortende wird zu *-i*

eas<u>y</u>   → eas<u>i</u>ly
funn<u>y</u>   → funn<u>i</u>ly

- auf einen Konsonanten folgendes *-le* wird zu *-ly*

simp<u>le</u>   → simp<u>ly</u>
probab<u>le</u>   → probab<u>ly</u>

- *-ic* am Wortende wird zu *-ically*

fantast<u>ic</u>   → fantast<u>ically</u>

Ausnahme:

pub<u>lic</u>   → public<u>ly</u>

Beachte:
- Unregelmäßig gebildet wird:

good   → well

- Endet das Adjektiv auf *-ly*, so kann kein Adverb gebildet werden; man verwendet deshalb: *in a* + Adjektiv + *manner/way*

friendly   → in a friendly manner

- In einigen Fällen haben Adjektiv und Adverb dieselbe Form, z. B.:

daily, early, fast, hard, long, low, weekly, yearly

- Manche Adjektive bilden zwei Adverbformen, die sich in der Bedeutung unterscheiden, z. B.:

Adj./Adv.	Adv. auf *-ly*
hard	*hardly*
schwierig, hart	kaum
late	*lately*
spät	neulich, kürzlich
near	*nearly*
nahe	beinahe

The task is <u>hard</u>. (adjective)
Die Aufgabe ist schwierig.
She works <u>hard</u>. (adverb)
Sie arbeitet hart.
She <u>hardly</u> works. (adverb)
Sie arbeitet kaum.

1

Verwendung
Adverbien bestimmen
- Verben,

She <u>easily</u> <u>found</u> her brother in the crowd.
Sie fand ihren Bruder leicht in der Menge.

- Adjektive,

This band is <u>extremely</u> <u>famous</u>.
Diese Band ist sehr berühmt.

- andere Adverbien oder

He walks <u>extremely</u> <u>quickly</u>.
Er geht äußerst schnell.

- einen ganzen Satz
näher.

<u>Fortunately</u>, <u>nobody was hurt</u>.
Glücklicherweise wurde niemand verletzt.

Beachte:
Nach bestimmten Verben, die einen
Zustand ausdrücken, steht nicht das
Adverb, sondern das Adjektiv, z. B.:

to be	sein
to become	werden
to get	werden
to seem	scheinen
to stay	bleiben

Everything <u>seems</u> <u>quiet</u>.
Alles scheint ruhig zu sein.

Nach manchen Verben kann ent-
weder ein Adjektiv oder ein Adverb
folgen (z. B. nach *to feel, to look, to
smell, to taste*). Mit Adverb
beschreiben diese Verben eine
Tätigkeit, mit Adjektiv eine
Eigenschaft des Subjekts.

Harry <u>looks</u> <u>happy</u>. (Eigenschaft)
Harry sieht glücklich aus.

Harry <u>looks</u> <u>happily</u> at his cake. (Tätigkeit)
Harry schaut glücklich auf seinen Kuchen.

Steigerung des Adjektivs – *Comparison of Adjectives*

Bildung
Man unterscheidet:
- Grundform / Positiv *(positive)*
- 1. Steigerungsform / Komparativ
  (comparative)
- 2. Steigerungsform / Superlativ
  (superlative)

Peter is <u>young</u>.

Jane is <u>younger</u>.

Paul is <u>the youngest</u>.

Steigerung auf *-er, -est*

- einsilbige Adjektive

  old, old<u>er</u>, old<u>est</u>
  alt, älter, am ältesten

- zweisilbige Adjektive, die auf
  -er, -le, -ow oder *-y* enden

  clever, clever<u>er</u>, clever<u>est</u>
  klug, klüger, am klügsten

  simple, simpl<u>er</u>, simpl<u>est</u>
  einfach, einfacher, am einfachsten

  narrow, narrow<u>er</u>, narrow<u>est</u>
  eng, enger, am engsten

  funny, funn<u>ier</u>, funn<u>iest</u>
  lustig, lustiger, am lustigsten

Beachte:

- stummes *-e* am Wortende entfällt

  simpl<u>e</u>, simpl<u>er</u>, simpl<u>est</u>

- nach einem Konsonanten wird
  -y am Wortende zu *-i-*

  funn<u>y</u>, funn<u>ier</u>, funn<u>iest</u>

- nach betontem Vokal wird ein
  Konsonant am Wortende verdoppelt

  fi<u>t</u>, fi<u>tt</u>er, fi<u>tt</u>est

Steigerung mit *more …, most …*

- zweisilbige Adjektive, die nicht
  auf *-er, -le, -ow* oder *-y* enden

  useful, <u>more</u> useful, <u>most</u> useful
  nützlich, nützlicher, am nützlichsten

- Adjektive mit drei und mehr
  Silben

  difficult, <u>more</u> difficult, <u>most</u> difficult
  schwierig, schwieriger, am schwierigsten

Unregelmäßige Steigerung

Die unregelmäßig gesteigerten
Adjektive muss man auswendig
lernen. Einige sind hier angegeben:

good, better, best

bad, worse, worst

many, more, most

much, more, most

little, less, least

Steigerungsformen im Satz – *Sentences with Comparisons*

Es gibt folgende Möglichkeiten,
Steigerungen im Satz zu verwenden:

- **Grundform:** Zwei oder mehr
  Personen oder Sachen sind
  gleich oder ungleich: *(not) as* +
  Grundform des Adjektivs + *as*

  Anne is <u>as</u> <u>tall</u> <u>as</u> John (and Sue).
  Anne ist genauso groß wie John (und Sue).
  John is <u>not as</u> <u>tall</u> <u>as</u> Steve.
  John ist nicht so groß wie Steve.

- **Komparativ:** Zwei oder mehr
  Personen/Sachen sind **verschie-**
  den (größer/besser …):
  Komparativ des Adjektivs + *than*

  Steve is <u>taller</u> <u>than</u> Anne.
  Steve ist größer als Anne.

- **Superlativ:** Eine Person/Sache
  wird besonders hervorgehoben
  (der/die/das größte/beste …):
  the + Superlativ des Adjektivs

  Steve is <u>the</u> <u>tallest</u> boy in class.
  Steve ist der größte Junge in der Klasse.

Steigerung des Adverbs – *Comparison of Adverbs*

Adverbien können wie Adjektive
auch gesteigert werden.

- Adverbien auf *-ly* werden mit
  more, most bzw. mit *less, least*
  gesteigert.

  She talks <u>more</u> <u>quickly</u> than John.
  Sie spricht schneller als John.

- Adverbien, die dieselbe Form
  wie das Adjektiv haben, werden
  mit *-er, -est* gesteigert.

  fast   – fast<u>er</u> – fast<u>est</u>
  early – earl<u>ier</u> – earl<u>iest</u>

- Manche Adverbien haben unregelmäßige Steigerungsformen,
  z. B.:

  well   – better – best
  badly – worse   – worst
  little – less   – least
  much – more   – most

Die Stellung von adverbialen Bestimmungen im Satz – *The Position of Adverbials in Sentences*

Adverbien und andere adverbiale
Bestimmungen können verschiedene Positionen im Satz einnehmen:

- Am **Anfang des Satzes**, vor dem Subjekt *(front position)*

Tomorrow he will be in London.
Morgen [betont] wird er in London sein.
Unfortunately, I can't come to the party.
Leider kann ich nicht zur Party kommen.

- **Im Satz** *(mid position)*
  vor dem Vollverb,

She often goes to school by bike.
Sie fährt oft mit dem Rad in die Schule.

nach *to be,*

She is already at home.
Sie ist schon zu Hause.

nach dem ersten Hilfsverb.

You can even go swimming there.
Man kann dort sogar schwimmen gehen.

- Am **Ende des Satzes**
  (end position)
  Gibt es mehrere Adverbien am Satzende, so gilt die **Reihenfolge**:
  Art und Weise – Ort – Zeit
  (manner – place – time)

He will be in London tomorrow.
Er wird morgen in London sein.
The snow melts slowly in the mountains at springtime.
Im Frühling schmilzt der Schnee langsam in den Bergen.

2 Pronomen und Begleiter – *Pronouns and Determiners*

Possessivpronomen und -begleiter – *Possessive Pronouns and Determiners*

„Possessiv" bedeutet **besitzanzeigend**. Man verwendet diese Formen, um zu sagen, **wem etwas gehört**. Man unterscheidet Possessivbegleiter, die mit einem Substantiv stehen, und Possessivpronomen (sie ersetzen ein Substantiv):

mit Substantiv	ohne Substantiv
my	*mine*
your	*yours*
his/her/its	*his/hers/–*
our	*ours*
your	*yours*
their	*theirs*

This is my bike. – This is mine.
This is your bike. – This is yours.
This is her bike. – This is hers.
This is our bike. – This is ours.
This is your bike. – This is yours.
This is their bike. – This is theirs.

Reflexivpronomen – *Reflexive Pronouns*

Reflexivpronomen *(reflexive pronouns)* **beziehen sich auf das Subjekt** des Satzes **zurück**. Es handelt sich also um dieselbe Person:

myself	I will look after <u>myself</u>.
yourself	<u>You</u> will look after <u>yourself</u>.
himself / herself / itself	<u>He</u> will look after <u>himself</u>.
ourselves	<u>We</u> will look after <u>ourselves</u>.
yourselves	<u>You</u> will look after <u>yourselves</u>.
themselves	<u>They</u> will look after <u>themselves</u>.

Beachte:

* Einige Verben stehen ohne Reflexivpronomen, obwohl im Deutschen mit „mich, dich, sich etc." übersetzt wird.

    I apologize …
    Ich entschuldige mich …
    He is hiding.
    Er versteckt <u>sich</u>.

* Einige Verben können sowohl mit einem Objekt als auch mit einem Reflexivpronomen verwendet werden. Dabei ändert sich die Bedeutung, z. B. bei *to control, to enjoy, to help, to occupy.*

    He is enjoying <u>the party</u>.
    Er genießt die Party.
    She is enjoying <u>herself</u>.
    Sie amüsiert sich.

    He is helping <u>the child</u>.
    Er hilft dem Kind.
    Help <u>yourself</u>!
    Bedienen Sie sich!

Reziprokes Pronomen – *Reciprocal Pronoun ("each other / one another")*

each other / one another ist unveränderlich. Es bezieht sich auf **zwei oder mehr Personen** und wird mit „sich (gegenseitig) / einander" übersetzt.

They looked at <u>each other</u> and laughed.
Sie schauten sich (gegenseitig) an und lachten.
oder:
Sie schauten einander an und lachten.

Beachte:
Einige Verben stehen ohne *each other*, obwohl im Deutschen mit „sich" übersetzt wird.

to meet	*sich treffen*
to kiss	*sich küssen*
to fall in love	*sich verlieben*

3 Präpositionen – *Prepositions*

Präpositionen *(prepositions)* drücken **räumliche, zeitliche oder andere Arten von Beziehungen** aus.

The ball is <u>under</u> the table.
He came home <u>after</u> six o'clock.

Die wichtigsten Präpositionen mit Beispielen für ihre Verwendung:

- *at*
  Ortsangabe: *at home*

  I'm <u>at home</u> now. *Ich bin jetzt zu Hause.*

  Zeitangabe: *at 3 p.m.*

  He arrived <u>at 3 p.m.</u> *Er kam um 15 Uhr an.*

- *by*
  Angabe des Mittels: *by bike*

  She went to work <u>by bike</u>.
  Sie fuhr mit dem Rad zur Arbeit.

  Angabe der Ursache: *by mistake*

  He did it <u>by mistake</u>.
  Er hat es aus Versehen getan.

  Zeitangabe: *by tomorrow*

  You will get the letter <u>by tomorrow</u>.
  Du bekommst den Brief bis morgen.

- *for*
  Zeitdauer: *for hours*

  We waited for the bus <u>for hours</u>.
  Wir warteten stundenlang auf den Bus.

- *from*
  Ortsangabe: *from Dublin*

  Ian is <u>from Dublin</u>.
  Ian kommt aus Dublin.

  Zeitangabe: *from nine to five*

  We work <u>from nine to five</u>.
  Wir arbeiten von neun bis fünf Uhr.

- *in*
  Ortsangabe: *in England*

  <u>In England</u>, they drive on the left.
  In England herrscht Linksverkehr.

  Zeitangabe: *in the morning*

  They woke up <u>in the morning</u>.
  Sie wachten am Morgen auf.

- *of*
  Ortsangabe: *north of the city*

  The village lies <u>north of the city</u>.
  Das Dorf liegt nördlich der Stadt.

- *on*
  Ortsangabe: *on the left,*
                 on the floor

  <u>On the left</u> you see the London Eye.
  Links sehen Sie das London Eye.

  Zeitangabe: *on Monday*

  <u>On Monday</u> she will buy the tickets.
  (Am) Montag kauft sie die Karten.

- *to*

  Richtungsangabe: *to the left*

  Angabe des Ziels: *to London*

Please turn <u>to the left</u>.
Bitte wenden Sie sich nach links.

He goes <u>to London</u> every year.
Er fährt jedes Jahr nach London.

4 Modale Hilfsverben – *Modal Auxiliaries*

Zu den **modalen Hilfsverben** *(modal auxiliaries)* zählen z. B. *can, may* und *must.*

Bildung

- Die modalen Hilfsverben haben für alle Personen **nur eine Form**: kein *-s* in der 3. Person Singular.

I, you, he/she/it,
we, you, they $\Big\}$ must

- Auf ein modales Hilfsverb folgt der **Infinitiv ohne *to***.

You <u>must</u> <u>listen</u> to my new record.
Du musst dir meine neue Platte anhören.

- **Frage und Verneinung** werden nicht mit *do/did* umschrieben.

<u>Can</u> you help me, please?
Kannst du mir bitte helfen?

Die modalen Hilfsverben können nicht alle Zeiten bilden. Deshalb benötigt man **Ersatzformen** (können auch im Präsens verwendet werden).

- *can* (können)
  Ersatzformen:
  (to) be able to (Fähigkeit),
  (to) be allowed to (Erlaubnis)

I <u>can</u> sing./I <u>was able to</u> sing.
Ich kann singen. / Ich konnte singen.

You <u>can't</u> go to the party./
I <u>wasn't allowed to</u> go to the party.
*Du darfst nicht auf die Party gehen./
Ich durfte nicht auf die Party gehen.*

Beachte: Im *simple past* und *conditional I* ist auch *could* möglich.

When I was three, I <u>could</u> already ski.
Mit drei konnte ich schon Ski fahren.

- *may* (dürfen) – sehr höflich
  Ersatzform: *(to) be allowed to*

You <u>may</u> go home early./
You <u>were allowed to</u> go home early.
Du darfst/durftest früh nach Hause gehen.

- *must* (müssen)
  Ersatzform: *(to) have to*

He <u>must</u> be home by ten o'clock./
He <u>had to</u> be home by ten o'clock.
Er muss/musste um zehn Uhr zu Hause sein.

You <u>must not</u> eat all the cake.
Du darfst nicht den ganzen Kuchen essen.

You <u>don't have to</u>/<u>needn't</u> eat all the cake.
Du musst nicht den ganzen Kuchen essen./
Du brauchst nicht … zu essen.

Infinitiv, Gerundium oder Partizip? – Die infiniten Verbformen

5 Infinitiv – *Infinitive*

Der **Infinitiv** (Grundform des
Verbs) **mit *to*** steht z. B. **nach**
- bestimmten **Verben**, z. B.:

to decide	(sich) entscheiden, beschließen
to expect	erwarten
to hope	hoffen
to manage	schaffen
to plan	planen
to promise	versprechen
to want	wollen

He <u>decided</u> <u>to wait</u>.
Er beschloss zu warten.

- bestimmten **Substantiven und Pronomen** *(something, anything)*, z. B.:

attempt	Versuch
idea	Idee
plan	Plan
wish	Wunsch

We haven't got <u>anything</u> <u>to eat</u> at home.
Wir haben nichts zu essen zu Hause.

It was her <u>plan</u> <u>to visit</u> him in May.
Sie hatte vor, ihn im Mai zu besuchen.

- bestimmten **Adjektiven** (auch in Verbindung mit *too*/*enough*) und deren Steigerungsformen, z. B.:

certain	sicher
difficult/hard	schwer, schwierig
easy	leicht

It was <u>difficult</u> <u>to follow</u> her.
Es war schwer, ihr zu folgen.

- **Fragewörtern**, wie z. B. *what, where, which, who, when, how* und nach *whether*. Diese Konstruktion ersetzt eine indirekte Frage mit modalem Hilfsverb.

We knew where to find her. / We knew where we would find her. *Wir wussten, wo wir sie finden würden.*

Die Konstruktion **Objekt + Infinitiv** wird im Deutschen oft mit einem „dass"-Satz übersetzt. Sie steht z. B. **nach**

- bestimmten **Verben**, z. B.:

to allow	erlauben
to get	veranlassen
to help	helfen
to persuade	überreden

She allowed him to go to the cinema. *Sie erlaubte ihm, dass er ins Kino geht. / ... ins Kino zu gehen.*

- **Verb + Präposition**, z. B.:

to count on	rechnen mit
to rely on	sich verlassen auf
to wait for	warten auf

She relies on him to arrive in time. *Sie verlässt sich darauf, dass er rechtzeitig ankommt.*

- **Adjektiv + Präposition**, z. B.:

easy for	leicht
necessary for	notwendig
nice of	nett
silly of	dumm

It is necessary for you to learn maths. *Es ist notwendig, dass du Mathe lernst.*

- **Substantiv + Präposition**, z. B.:

opportunity for	Gelegenheit
idea for	Idee
time for	Zeit

Work experience is a good opportunity for you to find out which job suits you. *Ein Praktikum ist eine gute Gelegenheit, herauszufinden, welcher Beruf zu dir passt.*

- einem **Adjektiv**, das durch *too* oder *enough* näher bestimmt wird.

The box is too heavy for me to carry. *Die Kiste ist mir zu schwer zum Tragen.*

The weather is good enough for us to go for a walk. *Das Wetter ist gut genug, dass wir spazieren gehen können.*

6 Gerundium (-*ing*-Form) – *Gerund*

Bildung
Infinitiv + -*ing*

read → reading

Beachte:
* stummes -*e* entfällt
* nach kurzem betontem Vokal:
  Schlusskonsonant verdoppelt
* -*ie* wird zu -*y*

write → writing
stop → stopping

lie → lying

Verwendung
Die -*ing*-Form steht nach bestimmten
Ausdrücken und kann verschiedene
Funktionen im Satz einnehmen, z. B.:

* als **Subjekt** des Satzes

Skiing is fun. *Skifahren macht Spaß.*

* nach bestimmten **Verben**
  (als **Objekt** des Satzes), z. B.:

to avoid	vermeiden
to enjoy	genießen, gern tun
to keep (on)	weitermachen
to miss	vermissen
to risk	riskieren
to suggest	vorschlagen

He enjoys reading comics.
Er liest gerne Comics.

You risk losing a friend.
Du riskierst, einen Freund zu verlieren.

* nach **Verb + Präposition**, z. B.:

to agree with	zustimmen
to believe in	glauben an
to dream of	träumen von
to look forward to	sich freuen auf
to talk about	sprechen über

She dreams of meeting a star.
Sie träumt davon, einen Star zu treffen.

* nach **Adjektiv + Präposition**,
  z. B.:

afraid of	sich fürchten vor
famous for	berühmt für
good/bad at	gut/schlecht in
interested in	interessiert an

He is afraid of losing his job.
Er hat Angst, seine Arbeit zu verlieren.

11

- nach **Substantiv + Präposition**, z. B.:

chance of	Chance, Aussicht	Do you have a <u>chance</u> <u>of</u> <u>getting</u> the job?
danger of	Gefahr	*Hast du Aussicht, die Stelle zu bekommen?*
reason for	Grund	
way of	Art und Weise	

- nach **Präpositionen** und **Konjunktionen der Zeit**, z. B.:

after	nachdem	
before	bevor	<u>Before</u> <u>leaving</u> the room he said goodbye.
by	indem,	*Bevor er den Raum verließ,*
	dadurch, dass	*verabschiedete er sich.*
in spite of	trotz	
instead of	statt	

7 Infinitiv oder Gerundium? – *Infinitive or Gerund?*

Einige Verben können sowohl **mit dem Infinitiv** als auch **mit der -*ing*-Form** stehen, **ohne** dass sich die **Bedeutung ändert**, z. B. *to love, to hate, to prefer, to start, to begin, to continue.*

I <u>hate</u> <u>getting up</u> early.
I <u>hate</u> <u>to get up</u> early.
Ich hasse es, früh aufzustehen.

Bei manchen Verben **ändert sich** jedoch die **Bedeutung**, je nachdem, ob sie mit Infinitiv oder mit der -*ing*-Form verwendet werden, z. B. *to remember, to forget, to stop.*

- *to remember* + Infinitiv:
  „daran denken, etwas zu tun"

  I must <u>remember</u> <u>to post</u> the invitations.
  Ich muss daran denken, die Einladungen einzuwerfen.

  to remember + *ing*-Form:
  „sich erinnern, etwas getan zu haben"

  I <u>remember</u> <u>posting</u> the invitations.
  Ich erinnere mich daran, die Einladungen eingeworfen zu haben.

- *to forget* + Infinitiv:
  „vergessen, etwas zu tun"

  to forget + *ing*-Form:
  „vergessen, etwas getan zu haben"

Don't <u>forget</u> <u>to water</u> the plants.
Vergiss nicht, die Pflanzen zu gießen.

I'll never <u>forget</u> <u>meeting</u> the President.
Ich werde nie vergessen, wie ich den Präsidenten traf.

- *to stop* + Infinitiv:
  „stehen bleiben, um etwas zu tun"

  to stop + *ing*-Form:
  „aufhören, etwas zu tun"

I <u>stopped</u> <u>to read</u> the road sign.
Ich hielt an, um das Verkehrsschild zu lesen.

He <u>stopped</u> <u>laughing</u>.
Er hörte auf zu lachen.

8 Partizipien – *Participles*

Partizip Präsens – *Present Participle*

Bildung
Infinitiv + *ing*
Sonderformen: siehe *gerund*
(S. 11)

talk → talking

Verwendung
Das *present participle* verwendet man:
- zur Bildung der Verlaufsform *present progressive,*
- zur Bildung der Verlaufsform *past progressive,*
- zur Bildung der Verlaufsform *present perfect progressive,*
- zur Bildung der Verlaufsform *future progressive,*
- wie ein Adjektiv, wenn es vor einem Substantiv steht.

Peter is <u>reading</u>.
Peter liest (gerade).

Peter was <u>reading</u> when I saw him.
Peter las (gerade), als ich ihn sah.

I have been <u>living</u> in Sydney for 5 years.
Ich lebe seit 5 Jahren in Sydney.

This time tomorrow I will be <u>working</u>.
Morgen um diese Zeit werde ich arbeiten.

The village hasn't got <u>running</u> water.
Das Dorf hat kein fließendes Wasser.

Partizip Perfekt – *Past Participle*

Bildung
Infinitiv + *-ed*   talk → talk<u>ed</u>

Beachte:
- stummes *-e* entfällt   liv<u>e</u> → liv<u>ed</u>
- nach betontem Vokal wird der   stop → sto<u>pp</u>ed
  Schlusskonsonant verdoppelt
- *-y* wird zu *-ie*   cry → cr<u>ie</u>d
- unregelmäßige Verben   be → been
  (S. 32 f.)

Verwendung
Das *past participle* verwendet man
- zur Bildung des *present perfect*,

  He hasn't <u>talked</u> to Tom yet.
  Er hat noch nicht mit Tom gesprochen.

- zur Bildung des *past perfect*,

  Before they went biking in France, they had <u>bought</u> new bikes.
  Bevor sie nach Frankreich zum Radfahren gingen, hatten sie neue Fahrräder gekauft.

- zur Bildung des *future perfect*,

  The letter will have <u>arrived</u> by then.
  Der Brief wird bis dann angekommen sein.

- zur Bildung des Passivs,

  The fish was <u>eaten</u> by the cat.
  Der Fisch wurde von der Katze gefressen.

- wie ein Adjektiv, wenn es vor einem Substantiv steht.

  Peter has got a well-<u>paid</u> job.
  Peter hat eine gut bezahlte Stelle.

Verkürzung eines Nebensatzes durch ein Partizip

Adverbiale Nebensätze (meist kausale oder temporale Bedeutung) und **Relativsätze** können durch ein Partizip verkürzt werden.

She watches the news because she wants to stay informed.
<u>Wanting</u> to stay informed, she watches the news.
Sie sieht sich die Nachrichten an, weil sie informiert bleiben möchte.

Das **Zeitverhältnis zwischen Haupt- und Nebensatz** bestimmt die Form des Partizips:

- Das *present participle* verwendet man, um Gleichzeitigkeit mit der Haupthandlung auszudrücken.

He did his homework <u>listening</u> to music.
Er machte seine Hausaufgaben und hörte dabei Musik.

- *Having + past participle* verwendet man, um auszudrücken, dass die Nebenhandlung vor der Haupthandlung geschah.

<u>Having done</u> his homework, he listened to music.
Nachdem er seine Hausaufgaben gemacht hatte, hörte er Musik.

- Das *past participle* verwendet man auch, um einen Satz im Passiv zu verkürzen.

Aisha is a manager in a five-star hotel <u>which</u> <u>is called</u> Pacific View.
Aisha is a manager in a five-star hotel <u>called</u> Pacific View.

Beachte:
- Man kann einen Temporal- oder Kausalsatz verkürzen, wenn **Haupt- und Nebensatz dasselbe Subjekt** haben.

When <u>he</u> was walking down the street, <u>he</u> saw Jo.
(When) <u>walking</u> down the street, <u>he</u> saw Jo.
Als er die Straße entlangging, sah er Jo.

- Bei **Kausalsätzen** entfallen die Konjunktionen *as, because* und *since* im verkürzten Nebensatz.

As <u>he</u> was hungry, <u>he</u> bought a sandwich.
<u>Being</u> hungry, <u>he</u> bought a sandwich.
Da er hungrig war, kaufte er ein Sandwich.

- In einem **Temporalsatz** bleibt die einleitende **Konjunktion** häufig erhalten, um dem Satz eine **eindeutige Bedeutung** zuzuweisen.

When <u>he</u> left, <u>he</u> forgot to lock the door.
<u>When</u> <u>leaving</u>, <u>he</u> forgot to lock the door.
Als er ging, vergaß er, die Tür abzuschließen.

Tara got sick <u>eating</u> too much chocolate.
Tara wurde schlecht, als/während/da sie zu viel Schokolade aß.

Die Vorzeitigkeit einer Handlung kann durch *after + present participle* oder durch *having + past participle* ausgedrückt werden.

<u>After</u> <u>finishing</u> / <u>Having finished</u> breakfast, he went to work.
Nachdem er sein Frühstück beendet hatte, ging er zur Arbeit.

• Bei **Relativsätzen** entfallen die Relativpronomen *who, which* und *that*.	I saw a six-year-old boy <u>who</u> pl<u>ayed</u> the piano. I saw a six-year-old boy pl<u>aying</u> the piano. *Ich sah einen sechsjährigen Jungen, der gerade Klavier spielte. / ... Klavier spielen.*

Verbindung von zwei Hauptsätzen durch ein Partizip

Zwei Hauptsätze können durch ein Partizip verbunden werden, wenn sie **dasselbe Subjekt** haben. **Beachte:** • Das Subjekt des zweiten Hauptsatzes und die Konjunktion *and* entfallen. • Die Verbform des zweiten Hauptsatzes wird durch das Partizip ersetzt.	<u>He</u> did his homework and <u>he</u> listened to the radio. <u>He</u> did his homework <u>listening</u> to the radio. *Er machte seine Hausaufgaben und hörte Radio.*

Bildung und Gebrauch der finiten Verbformen

9 Zeiten – *Tenses*

Simple Present

Bildung Infinitiv, Ausnahme 3. Person Singular: Infinitiv + *-s*	stand – he/she/it stand<u>s</u>
Beachte: • Bei Verben, die auf *-s, -sh, -ch, -x* und *-z* enden, wird in der 3. Person Singular *-es* angefügt.	kiss – he/she/it kiss<u>es</u> ru<u>sh</u> – he/she/it rush<u>es</u> teach – he/she/it teach<u>es</u> fi<u>x</u> – he/she/it fix<u>es</u>
• Bei Verben, die auf Konsonant + *-y* enden, wird *-es* angefügt; *-y* wird zu *-i-*.	car<u>ry</u> – he/she/it carr<u>ies</u>

Bildung von Fragen im *simple present*
(Fragewort +) *do/does* + Subjekt +
Infinitiv

Where <u>does</u> he <u>live</u>? /
<u>Does</u> he <u>live</u> in London?
Wo lebt er? / Lebt er in London?

Beachte:
Die Umschreibung mit *do/does*
wird nicht verwendet,
- wenn nach dem Subjekt gefragt
  wird (mit *who, what, which*),

<u>Who</u> <u>comes</u> to the party?
Wer kommt zur Party?

<u>Which</u> tree <u>has</u> more leaves?
Welcher Baum hat mehr Blätter?

- wenn die Frage mit *is/are* oder
  einem Hilfsverb gebildet wird.

<u>Are</u> you happy?
Bist du glücklich?

<u>Can</u> you help me?
Können Sie mir helfen?

**Bildung der Verneinung im
*simple present***
don't/doesn't + Infinitiv

He <u>doesn't like</u> football.
Er mag Fußball nicht.

Verwendung
Das *simple present* wird verwendet:
- bei Tätigkeiten, die man
  gewohnheitsmäßig oder häufig
  ausführt
  Signalwörter: z. B. *always, often,
  never, every day, every morning,
  every afternoon*

Every morning John <u>buys</u> a newspaper.
Jeden Morgen kauft John eine Zeitung.

- bei **allgemeingültigen** Aussagen

London <u>is</u> a big city.
London ist eine große Stadt.

I like science-fiction films.
Ich mag Science-Fiction-Filme.

- bei **Zustandsverben**: Sie drücken
  Eigenschaften / Zustände von Personen und Dingen aus und stehen
  normalerweise nur in der *simple
  form*, z. B. *to hate, to know, to
  like.*

Present Progressive / Present Continuous

Bildung
am/is/are + present participle

read → <u>am/is/are</u> <u>reading</u>

Bildung von Fragen im *present progressive*
(Fragewort +) *am/is/are* + Subjekt + *present participle*

<u>Is</u> <u>Peter</u> <u>reading</u>?/<u>What</u> <u>is</u> <u>he</u> <u>reading</u>?
Liest Peter gerade?/Was liest er?

Bildung der Verneinung im *present progressive*
am not/isn't/aren't + present participle

Peter <u>isn't</u> <u>reading</u>.
Peter liest gerade nicht.

Verwendung
Mit dem *present progressive* drückt man aus, dass etwas **gerade passiert** und **noch nicht abgeschlossen** ist. Es wird daher auch als **Verlaufsform** der Gegenwart bezeichnet.

Signalwörter: *at the moment, now*

At the moment, Peter <u>is drinking</u> a cup of tea.
Im Augenblick trinkt Peter eine Tasse Tee.
[Er hat damit angefangen und noch nicht aufgehört.]

Simple Past

Bildung
Regelmäßige Verben: Infinitiv + *-ed*

walk → walk<u>ed</u>

Beachte:
* stummes *-e* entfällt

hop<u>e</u> → hop<u>ed</u>

* Bei Verben, die auf Konsonant + *-y* enden, wird *-y* zu *-i-*.

carr<u>y</u> → carr<u>ied</u>

* Nach betontem Vokal wird der Schlusskonsonant verdoppelt.

sto<u>p</u> → sto<u>pped</u>

Unregelmäßige Verben: siehe Liste S. 32 f.

be → was
have → had

Bildung von Fragen im *simple past*
(Fragewort +) *did* + Subjekt + Infinitiv

(<u>Why</u>) <u>Did</u> <u>he</u> <u>look</u> out of the window?
(Warum) Sah er aus dem Fenster?

18

Beachte:
Die Umschreibung mit *did* wird nicht verwendet,

- wenn nach dem Subjekt gefragt wird (mit *who, what, which*),

Who paid the bill?
Wer zahlte die Rechnung?

What happened to your friend?
Was ist mit deinem Freund passiert?

- wenn die Frage mit *was/were* oder einem Hilfsverb gebildet wird.

Were you happy?
Warst du glücklich?

Could you watch the film?
Konntest du dir den Film ansehen?

Bildung der Verneinung im
simple past
did not/didn't + Infinitiv

He didn't call me.
Er rief mich nicht an.

Verwendung
Das *simple past* beschreibt Handlungen und Ereignisse, die **in der Vergangenheit passierten** und **bereits abgeschlossen** sind.

Signalwörter: z. B. *yesterday, last week/year, two years ago, in 2017*

Last week, he helped me with my homework.
Letzte Woche half er mir bei meinen Hausaufgaben.
[Die Handlung fand in der letzten Woche statt, ist also abgeschlossen.]

Past Progressive / Past Continuous

Bildung
was/were + *present participle*

watch → was/were watching

Verwendung
Die **Verlaufsform** *past progressive* verwendet man, wenn **zu einem bestimmten Zeitpunkt** in der Vergangenheit eine **Handlung ablief**, bzw. wenn eine **Handlung** von einer anderen **unterbrochen** wurde.

Yesterday at 9 o'clock I was still sleeping.
Gestern um 9 Uhr schlief ich noch.

I was reading a book when Peter came into the room.
Ich las (gerade) ein Buch, als Peter ins Zimmer kam.

Present Perfect (Simple)

Bildung
have/has + past participle

write ➜ <u>has/have</u> <u>written</u>

Verwendung
Das *present perfect* verwendet man,
- wenn ein Vorgang **in der Vergangenheit begonnen** hat
  und **noch andauert**,

- wenn das Ergebnis einer vergangenen Handlung **Auswirkungen
  auf die Gegenwart** hat.

Signalwörter: z. B. *already, ever,
just, how long, not … yet, since, for*

He <u>has lived</u> in London since 2008.
Er lebt seit 2008 in London.
[Er lebt jetzt immer noch in London.]

I <u>have</u> just <u>cleaned</u> my car.
Ich habe gerade mein Auto geputzt.
[Man sieht evtl. das saubere Auto.]

Have you <u>ever</u> been to Dublin?
Warst du schon jemals in Dublin?

Beachte:
- *have/has* können zu *'ve/'s*
  verkürzt werden.

- Das *present perfect* wird oft mit
  since und *for* verwendet („seit").
  - *since* gibt einen **Zeitpunkt** an:

  - *for* gibt einen **Zeitraum** an:

He<u>'s</u> given me his umbrella.
Er hat mir seinen Regenschirm gegeben.

Ron has lived in Sydney <u>since 2007</u>.
Ron lebt seit 2007 in Sydney.

Sally has lived in Berlin <u>for five years</u>.
Sally lebt seit fünf Jahren in Berlin.

Present Perfect Progressive / Present Perfect Continuous

Bildung
have/has + been + present participle

write ➜ <u>has/have</u> <u>been</u> <u>writing</u>

Verwendung
Die **Verlaufsform** *present perfect
progressive* verwendet man, um die
Dauer einer Handlung zu **betonen**, die in der Vergangenheit
begonnen hat und noch andauert.

She <u>has been sleeping</u> for ten hours.
Sie schläft seit zehn Stunden.

Past Perfect (Simple)

Bildung
had + past participle

write ➔ <u>had</u> <u>written</u>

Verwendung
Die Vorvergangenheit *past perfect* verwendet man, wenn ein Vorgang in der Vergangenheit **vor einem anderen Vorgang in der Vergangenheit abgeschlossen** wurde.

He <u>had bought</u> a ticket before he took the train to Manchester.
Er hatte eine Fahrkarte gekauft, bevor er den Zug nach Manchester nahm. [Beim Einsteigen war der Kauf abgeschlossen.]

Past Perfect Progressive / Past Perfect Continuous

Bildung
had + been + present participle

write ➔ <u>had</u> <u>been</u> <u>writing</u>

Verwendung
Die **Verlaufsform** *past perfect progressive* verwendet man für **Handlungen**, die in der Vergangenheit **bis zu dem Zeitpunkt andauerten**, zu dem eine neue Handlung einsetzte.

She <u>had been sleeping</u> for ten hours when the doorbell rang.
Sie hatte seit zehn Stunden geschlafen, als es an der Tür klingelte.
[Das Schlafen dauerte bis zu dem Zeitpunkt an, als es an der Tür klingelte.]

Will-future

Bildung
will + Infinitiv

buy ➔ <u>will</u> <u>buy</u>

Bildung von Fragen im *will-future*
(Fragewort +) *will* + Subjekt + Infinitiv

What <u>will</u> <u>you</u> <u>buy</u>?
Was wirst du kaufen?

Bildung der Verneinung im *will-future*
will not/won't + Infinitiv

Why <u>won't</u> you <u>come</u> to our party?
Warum kommst du nicht zu unserer Party?

Verwendung

Das *will-future* verwendet man, wenn ein Vorgang **in der Zukunft stattfinden** wird:

- bei Vorhersagen oder Vermutungen,

- bei spontanen Entscheidungen.

The weather will be fine tomorrow.
Das Wetter wird morgen schön (sein).

[doorbell] "I'll open the door."
"Ich werde die Tür öffnen."

Signalwörter: z. B. *tomorrow, next week, next Monday, next year, in three years, soon*

Going-to-future

Bildung

am/is/are + *going to* + Infinitiv

find → am/is/are going to find

Verwendung

Das *going-to-future* verwendet man, wenn man ausdrücken will:

- was man für die Zukunft **plant** oder **zu tun beabsichtigt**.

- dass ein **Ereignis bald eintreten wird**, da bestimmte **Anzeichen** vorhanden sind.

I am going to work in England this summer.
Diesen Sommer werde ich in England arbeiten.

Look at those clouds. It's going to rain soon.
Schau dir diese Wolken an. Es wird bald regnen.

Simple Present und *Present Progressive* zur Wiedergabe der Zukunft

Verwendung

- Mit dem *present progressive* drückt man **Pläne** für die Zukunft aus, für die bereits **Vorkehrungen** getroffen wurden.

We are flying to New York tomorrow.
Morgen fliegen wir nach New York.
[Wir haben schon Tickets.]

22

- Mit dem *simple present* wird ein zukünftiges Geschehen wiedergegeben, das **von außen festgelegt** wurde, z. B. Fahrpläne, Programme, Kalender.

The train <u>leaves</u> at 8.15 a.m.
Der Zug fährt um 8.15 Uhr.

The play <u>ends</u> at 10 p.m.
Das Theaterstück endet um 22 Uhr.

Future Progressive / Future Continuous

Bildung
will + be + present participle

work → <u>will</u> <u>be</u> <u>working</u>

Verwendung
Die **Verlaufsform** *future progressive* drückt aus, dass ein **Vorgang** in der Zukunft zu einem bestimmten Zeitpunkt **gerade ablaufen wird**.

Signalwörter: *this time next week / tomorrow, tomorrow* + Zeitangabe

This time tomorrow I <u>will</u> <u>be</u> <u>sitting</u> in a plane to London.
Morgen um diese Zeit werde ich gerade im Flugzeug nach London sitzen.

Future Perfect (Future II)

Bildung
will + have + past participle

go → <u>will</u> <u>have</u> <u>gone</u>

Verwendung
Das *future perfect* drückt aus, dass ein **Vorgang** in der Zukunft **abgeschlossen sein wird** (Vorzeitigkeit in der Zukunft).

Signalwörter: *by then, by* + Zeitangabe

By 5 p.m. tomorrow I <u>will</u> <u>have</u> <u>arrived</u> in London.
Morgen Nachmittag um fünf Uhr werde ich bereits in London angekommen sein.

Bildung

Form von *(to) be* in der entsprechenden Zeitform + *past participle*

The bridge <u>was</u> <u>finished</u> in 1894.
Die Brücke wurde 1894 fertiggestellt.

Zeitformen:

- *simple present*

  Aktiv: Joe <u>buys</u> the milk.
  Passiv: The milk <u>is</u> <u>bought</u> by Joe.

- *simple past*

  Aktiv: Joe <u>bought</u> the milk.
  Passiv: The milk <u>was</u> <u>bought</u> by Joe.

- *present perfect*

  Aktiv: Joe <u>has</u> <u>bought</u> the milk.
  Passiv: The milk <u>has been</u> <u>bought</u> by Joe.

- *past perfect*

  Aktiv: Joe <u>had bought</u> the milk.
  Passiv: The milk <u>had been</u> <u>bought</u> by Joe.

- *will-future*

  Aktiv: Joe <u>will buy</u> the milk.
  Passiv: The milk <u>will be</u> <u>bought</u> by Joe.

- *future perfect (future II)*

  Aktiv: Joe <u>will have bought</u> the milk.
  Passiv: The milk <u>will have been</u> <u>bought</u>
  by Joe.

- *conditional I*

  Aktiv: Joe <u>would buy</u> the milk.
  Passiv: The milk <u>would be</u> <u>bought</u> by Joe.

- *conditional II*

  Aktiv: Joe <u>would have</u> <u>bought</u> the milk.
  Passiv: The milk <u>would have been</u>
  <u>bought</u> by Joe.

Aktiv → Passiv

- Das Subjekt des Aktivsatzes wird zum Objekt des Passivsatzes. Es wird mit *by* angeschlossen.
- Das Objekt des Aktivsatzes wird zum Subjekt des Passivsatzes.

Aktiv: <u>Joe</u>   buys   <u>the milk</u>.
    Subjekt   *Objekt*

Passiv: <u>The milk</u> is bought <u>by Joe</u>.
    Subjekt   *by-agent*

- Stehen im Aktiv **zwei Objekte**, lassen sich zwei verschiedene Passivsätze bilden. Ein Objekt wird zum Subjekt des Passiv-satzes, das zweite bleibt Objekt.

Aktiv: They   gave   <u>her</u>   <u>a ball</u>.
    Subjekt   *ind. Obj.* *dir. Obj.*

Passiv: <u>She</u>   was given   <u>a ball</u>.
    Subjekt   *dir. Obj.*

Beachte:
Das indirekte Objekt muss im Passivsatz mit *to* angeschlossen werden.

oder:

Aktiv: They   gave   <u>her</u>   <u>a ball</u>.
        Subjekt   *ind. Obj.* *dir. Obj.*

Passiv: <u>A ball</u> was given   <u>to her</u>.
        Subjekt   *ind. Obj.*

Passiv → Aktiv

- Der mit *by* angeschlossene Handelnde *(by-agent)* des Passivsatzes wird zum Subjekt des Aktivsatzes; *by* entfällt.
- Das Subjekt des Passivsatzes wird zum Objekt des Aktivsatzes.
- Fehlt im Passivsatz der *by-agent*, muss im Aktivsatz ein Handelnder als Subjekt ergänzt werden, z. B. *somebody, we, you, they.*

Passiv: <u>The milk</u> is bought <u>by Joe</u>.
        Subjekt   *by-agent*

Aktiv: <u>Joe</u>   buys   <u>the milk.</u>
        Subjekt   *Objekt*

Passiv: <u>The match</u> was won.
        Subjekt

Aktiv: <u>They</u>   won   <u>the match.</u>
      (ergänztes)   *Objekt*
      Subjekt

Der Satz im Englischen

11 Wortstellung – *Word Order*

Im Aussagesatz gilt die Wortstellung <u>S</u>ubjekt – <u>P</u>rädikat – <u>O</u>bjekt *(subject – verb – object):*

- <u>Subjekt</u>: Wer oder was tut etwas?
- <u>Prädikat</u>: Was wird getan?
- <u>Objekt</u>: Worauf / Auf wen bezieht sich die Tätigkeit?

Für die Position von Orts- und Zeitangaben vgl. S. 4 f.

<u>Cats</u> <u>catch</u> <u>mice</u>.
Katzen fangen Mäuse.

12 Konditionalsätze – *Conditional Sentences*

Ein Konditionalsatz (Bedingungs-
satz) besteht aus zwei Teilen:
einem Nebensatz *(if-clause)* und
einem Hauptsatz *(main clause)*. Im
if-Satz steht die **Bedingung**
(condition), unter der die im
Hauptsatz genannte **Folge**
eintritt. Man unterscheidet drei
Arten von Konditionalsätzen:

Konditionalsatz Typ I

Bildung

* *if*-Satz (Bedingung):
  simple present

* Hauptsatz (Folge):
  will-future

If you <u>read</u> this book,
Wenn du dieses Buch liest,

you <u>will learn</u> a lot about music.
erfährst du eine Menge über Musik.

Der *if*-Satz kann auch nach dem
Hauptsatz stehen. In diesem Fall
entfällt das Komma:

* Hauptsatz: *will-future*

* *if*-Satz: *simple present*

You <u>will learn</u> a lot about music
Du erfährst eine Menge über Musik,

if you <u>read</u> this book.
wenn du dieses Buch liest.

Im Hauptsatz kann auch
* ein modales Hilfsverb (z. B. *can,
  must, may)* + Infinitiv sowie

* die Befehlsform des Verbs
  (Imperativ)
stehen.

If you go to London, you <u>must</u> <u>visit</u> me.
*Wenn du nach London fährst, musst du
mich besuchen.*

If it rains, <u>take</u> an umbrella.
*Wenn es regnet, nimm einen Schirm
mit.*

Verwendung
Bedingungssätze vom Typ I verwendet man, wenn die **Bedingung erfüllbar** ist. Man gibt an, was unter bestimmten Bedingungen **geschieht** oder **geschehen kann**.

Sonderform
Bedingungssätze vom Typ I verwendet man auch bei einer **generellen Regel**. Hierbei steht sowohl im Hauptsatz als auch im *if*-Satz das *simple present*.

If you <u>mix</u> blue and yellow, you <u>get</u> green.
Wenn du die Farbe Blau mit Gelb mischst, erhältst du Grün.

Konditionalsatz Typ II

Bildung
- *if*-Satz (Bedingung): *simple past*

- Hauptsatz (Folge): *conditional I = would* + Infinitiv

If I <u>went</u> to London,
Wenn ich nach London fahren würde,

I <u>would visit</u> the Tower.
würde ich mir den Tower ansehen.

Verwendung
Bedingungssätze vom Typ II verwendet man, wenn die **Bedingung nur theoretisch erfüllt** werden kann oder **nicht erfüllbar** ist.

Konditionalsatz Typ III

Bildung
- *if*-Satz (Bedingung): *past perfect*

- Hauptsatz (Folge): *conditional II = would* + *have* + *past participle*

If I <u>had gone</u> to London,
Wenn ich nach London gefahren wäre,

I <u>would have visited</u> the Tower of London.
hätte ich mir den Tower of London angesehen.

13 Relativsätze – *Relative Clauses*

Ein Relativsatz ist ein Nebensatz,
der sich **auf eine Person oder
Sache** des Hauptsatzes **bezieht** und
diese **näher beschreibt**:

The boy <u>who looks like Jane</u> is her
brother.
*Der Junge, der Jane ähnlich sieht,
ist ihr Bruder.*

- Hauptsatz:
- Relativsatz:

The boy … is her brother.
… who looks like Jane …

Bildung
Haupt- und Nebensatz werden
durch das Relativpronomen
verbunden.

- Das Relativpronomen *who*
  bezieht sich auf Personen.

Peter, <u>who</u> lives in London,
likes travelling.
Peter, der in London lebt, reist gerne.

- Das Relativpronomen *whose*
  (Genitiv) bezieht sich ebenfalls
  auf Personen. Es gibt die
  Zugehörigkeit dieser Person zu
  einer anderen Person oder Sache
  an.

Sam, <u>whose</u> mother is an architect,
is in my class.
*Sam, dessen Mutter Architektin ist,
geht in meine Klasse.*

- Auch *whom* (Akkusativ) bezieht
  sich auf **Personen**.

Anne, <u>whom</u>/<u>who</u> I like, is French.
Anne, die ich mag, ist Französin.

- Das Relativpronomen *which*
  bezieht sich auf **Sachen**.

The film "Dark Moon", <u>which</u> we
saw yesterday, was far too long.
*Der Film „Dark Moon", den wir
gestern sahen, war viel zu lang.*

- Das Relativpronomen *that* kann sich auf **Sachen** und auf **Personen** beziehen und wird nur verwendet, wenn die **Information** im Relativsatz **notwendig** ist, um den ganzen Satz zu verstehen.

The film <u>that</u> we saw last week was much better.
Der Film, den wir letzte Woche sahen, war viel besser.

Verwendung
Mithilfe von Relativpronomen kann man **zwei Sätze miteinander verbinden**.

<u>London</u> is England's biggest city.
<u>London</u> is very popular with tourists.
London ist Englands größte Stadt.
London ist bei Touristen sehr beliebt.

<u>London</u>, which is England's biggest city, is very popular with tourists.
London, die größte Stadt Englands, ist bei Touristen sehr beliebt.

Beachte:
Man unterscheidet zwei Arten von Relativsätzen:
- **Notwendige Relativsätze** (*defining relative clauses*) enthalten Informationen, die **für das Verständnis** des Satzes **erforderlich** sind.

The man <u>who is wearing a red shirt</u> is Mike.
Der Mann, der ein rotes Hemd trägt, ist Mike.

  Hier kann das Relativpronomen entfallen, wenn es Objekt ist; man spricht dann auch von *contact clauses*.

The book (<u>that</u>) I bought yesterday is thrilling.
Das Buch, das ich gestern gekauft habe, ist spannend.

- **Nicht notwendige Relativsätze** (*non-defining relative clauses*) enthalten **zusätzliche Informationen** zum Bezugswort, die für das Verständnis des Satzes nicht unbedingt notwendig sind. Dieser Typ von Relativsatz wird **mit Kommas** abgetrennt.

Sally, who went to a party yesterday, is very tired.
Sally, die gestern auf einer Party war, ist sehr müde.

14 Indirekte Rede – *Reported Speech*

Die indirekte Rede verwendet man, um **wiederzugeben, was ein anderer gesagt** oder **gefragt hat**.

Bildung
Um die indirekte Rede zu bilden, benötigt man ein **Einleitungsverb**. Häufig verwendete Einleitungsverben sind:

to say, to tell, to add, to mention, to think, to ask, to want to know, to answer

In der indirekten Rede verändern sich die **Pronomen**, in bestimmten Fällen auch die **Zeiten** und die **Orts-** und **Zeitangaben**.

- Wie die Pronomen sich verändern, hängt vom jeweiligen **Kontext** ab.

direkte Rede	indirekte Rede
Bob says to Jenny: "I like y<u>ou</u>."	Jenny tells Liz: "Bob says that he likes <u>me</u>."
Bob sagt zu Jenny: „Ich mag dich."	*Jenny erzählt Liz: „Bob sagt, dass er mich mag."*
Aber:	Jenny tells Liz that Bob likes <u>her</u>.
	Jenny erzählt Liz, dass Bob sie mag.

- **Zeiten:**
  Keine Veränderung, wenn das Einleitungsverb
  im *simple present* oder
  im *present perfect* steht:

direkte Rede	indirekte Rede
Bob <u>says</u>, "I <u>love</u> dancing."	Bob <u>says</u> (that) he <u>loves</u> dancing.
Bob sagt: „Ich tanze sehr gerne."	*Bob sagt, er tanze sehr gerne.*

In folgenden Fällen wird die Zeit der direkten Rede in der indirekten Rede **um eine Zeitstufe zurückversetzt**, wenn das **Einleitungsverb** im *simple past* steht:

Bob <u>said</u>, "I <u>love</u> dancing."	Bob <u>said</u> (that) he <u>loved</u> dancing.
Bob sagte: „Ich tanze sehr gerne."	*Bob sagte, er tanze sehr gerne.*

simple present	→	*simple past*	
simple past	→	*past perfect*	
present perfect	→	*past perfect*	
will-future	→	*conditional I*	

Joe: "I <u>like</u> it." Joe said he <u>liked</u> it.
Joe: "I <u>liked</u> it." Joe said he <u>had</u> <u>liked</u> it.
Joe: "I'<u>ve liked</u> it." Joe said he <u>had</u> <u>liked</u> it.
Joe: "I <u>will like</u> it." Joe said he <u>would</u> <u>like</u> it.

- **Zeitangaben** verändern sich, wenn der Bericht zu einem späteren Zeitpunkt erfolgt, z. B.:

- Welche **Ortsangabe** verwendet wird, hängt davon ab, wo sich der Sprecher im Moment befindet.

now	→	then, at that time
today	→	that day, yesterday
yesterday	→	the day before
the day before yesterday	→	two days before
tomorrow	→	the following day
next week	→	the following week
here	→	there

Bildung der indirekten Frage
Häufige Einleitungsverben für die indirekte Frage sind:

to ask, to want to know, to wonder

- **Fragewörter** bleiben in der indirekten Rede **erhalten**. Die **Umschreibung** mit *do/does/did* **entfällt** in der indirekten Frage.

Tom: "<u>When did</u> they arrive?" Tom asked <u>when</u> they had arrived.
Tom: „Wann sind sie angekommen?" *Tom fragte, wann sie angekommen seien.*

- Enthält die direkte Frage **kein Fragewort**, wird die indirekte Frage mit *whether* oder *if* eingeleitet:

Tom: "Are they staying at the hotel?" Tom asked <u>if/ whether</u> they were staying at the hotel.
Tom: „Übernachten sie im Hotel?" *Tom fragte, ob sie im Hotel übernachten.*

Befehle/Aufforderungen in der indirekten Rede
Häufige Einleitungsverben sind:

to tell, to order, to ask

In der indirekten Rede steht hier **Einleitungsverb + Objekt + (*not*) to + Infinitiv**.

Tom: "Leave the room." Tom <u>told</u> <u>me</u> <u>to</u> <u>leave</u> the room.
Tom: „Verlass den Raum." *Tom forderte mich auf, den Raum zu verlassen.*

Anhang

15 Liste wichtiger unregelmäßiger Verben – *List of Irregular Verbs*

Infinitive	Simple Past	Past Participle	*Deutsch*
be	was / were	been	*sein*
become	became	become	*werden*
begin	began	begun	*beginnen*
blow	blew	blown	*wehen, blasen*
break	broke	broken	*brechen*
bring	brought	brought	*bringen*
build	built	built	*bauen*
buy	bought	bought	*kaufen*
catch	caught	caught	*fangen*
choose	chose	chosen	*wählen*
come	came	come	*kommen*
cut	cut	cut	*schneiden*
do	did	done	*tun*
draw	drew	drawn	*zeichnen*
drink	drank	drunk	*trinken*
drive	drove	driven	*fahren*
eat	ate	eaten	*essen*
fall	fell	fallen	*fallen*
feed	fed	fed	*füttern*
feel	felt	felt	*fühlen*
find	found	found	*finden*
fly	flew	flown	*fliegen*
get	got	got	*bekommen*
give	gave	given	*geben*
go	went	gone	*gehen*
grow	grew	grown	*wachsen*
hang	hung	hung	*hängen*
have	had	had	*haben*
hear	heard	heard	*hören*
hit	hit	hit	*schlagen*
hold	held	held	*halten*
keep	kept	kept	*behalten*
know	knew	known	*wissen*

Infinitive	Simple Past	Past Participle	*Deutsch*
lay	laid	laid	*legen*
leave	left	left	*verlassen*
let	let	let	*lassen*
lie	lay	lain	*liegen*
lose	lost	lost	*verlieren*
make	made	made	*machen*
meet	met	met	*treffen*
pay	paid	paid	*bezahlen*
put	put	put	*stellen/setzen*
read	read	read	*lesen*
ring	rang	rung	*läuten/anrufen*
run	ran	run	*rennen*
say	said	said	*sagen*
see	saw	seen	*sehen*
sell	sold	sold	*verkaufen*
send	sent	sent	*schicken*
show	showed	shown	*zeigen*
sing	sang	sung	*singen*
sit	sat	sat	*sitzen*
sleep	slept	slept	*schlafen*
smell	smelt	smelt	*riechen*
speak	spoke	spoken	*sprechen*
spend	spent	spent	*ausgeben/ verbringen*
stand	stood	stood	*stehen*
steal	stole	stolen	*stehlen*
swim	swam	swum	*schwimmen*
take	took	taken	*nehmen*
teach	taught	taught	*lehren*
tell	told	told	*erzählen*
think	thought	thought	*denken*
throw	threw	thrown	*werfen*
wake	woke	woken	*aufwachen*
wear	wore	worn	*tragen (Kleidung)*
win	won	won	*gewinnen*
write	wrote	written	*schreiben*

20 minutes

Home schooling – as numbers increase, past stereotypes don't apply anymore (Track 1)

I **Multiple choice** (4 pts)

You are going to listen to an American radio show on the topic of home schooling. Decide which of the following statements is correct.

1. Home schooling …

   ☐ means that children do not go to public or private schools but are taught by their parents or private tutors.

   ☐ means that parents disapprove of the public and private school system.

   ☐ is not legal in the USA or Great Britain.

2. Liz is positive about being home schooled because she …

   ☐ has a lot of free time.

   ☐ can learn at her own pace.

   ☐ could not imagine being in a normal classroom.

3. Sceptics assume that home-schooled children are …

   ☐ not able to integrate into society.

   ☐ educationally ill-prepared.

   ☐ not religiously educated.

4. Home-schooled children …

   ☐ have more problems at schools of higher learning.

   ☐ are preferred by employers because of their initiative and sense of responsibility.

   ☐ do not have a reputation for reliability.

II Questions on the text (12 pts)

Listen to the radio show again, take notes on the following questions and then answer in full sentences.

1. Explain why Sarah decided to home school her children.

_____

_____

_____

_____

_____

_____

2. State four more possible reasons from the text why parents educate their children at home.

_____

_____

_____

_____

_____

_____

_____

_____

3. Describe the possible problems that can arise where home schooling is not successful.

_____

_____

_____

_____

_____

_____

Solution

Home schooling (Tapescript)

*✎ **Hinweis:** Lies dir alle Fragen und Aufgaben gründlich durch, **bevor** der Text zum
✎ ersten Mal vorgespielt wird, sodass du ungefähr weißt, worum es in dem Text
✎ geht und worauf du achten musst. Richte deine Aufmerksamkeit beim ersten An-
✎ hören auf den Gesamtzusammenhang des Textes. Es macht nichts, wenn du nicht
✎ jedes einzelne Wort verstehst. Mach dir bereits Notizen zu den Fragen, wenn du
✎ dem Text entsprechende Informationen entnehmen kannst. Bevor der Text zum
✎ zweiten Mal vorgespielt wird, schau dir an, welche Informationen dir noch fehlen,
✎ damit du dich auf die entsprechenden Textstellen konzentrieren kannst. Nimm dir
✎ nach dem zweiten Anhören genug Zeit, um anhand deiner Notizen sorgfältig voll-
✎ ständige Sätze zu formulieren.*

RADIO PRESENTER: Hi there, this is Paul Smith on behalf of RadioToday. Our topic
today is "Home schooling", which is quite interesting since the number of children
taught at home has increased steadily over the last few years. My guests today are:
Sarah Jenkins, who decided to teach her daughter at home …

SARAH: Hello, Paul, nice to be here.

RADIO PRESENTER: … and Liz, her fifteen-year-old daughter, who will give us her
opinion on home schooling …

LIZ: Hi, it's great to be here.

RADIO PRESENTER: … and Nelson Rodriguez, an expert for home schooling in the
US and abroad. Welcome to all of you.

NELSON: Thanks for the invitation.

RADIO PRESENTER: Nelson, for those of us who have no experience at all as far as
home schooling is concerned, could you just briefly explain what it actually is?

NELSON: Of course. Well, home schooling, which is also called home education,
means that children are educated at home by their parents or by tutors rather than
in public or private schools. In some countries, such as the US or Great Britain,
home schooling is legal, so parents can opt out of the public and private education
system and choose to provide their children with an alternative learning environment.

RADIO PRESENTER: Home schooling appears to be growing ever more popular.
Sarah, what were your reasons to home school your children?

SARAH: Well, I'm not at all against our education system. I'm convinced that most
of the teachers at our schools do a great job and work hard for the instruction of
our children. It's just that I think they advance too quickly. I wanted my children
to learn at their own pace and be taught according to their abilities. I felt that the
individual attention my children receive at home will take their personal needs
into account and help them to learn more successfully. I was also worried about

violence at school and negative peer pressure, as far as drugs and alcohol are concerned. And I also saw the chance of spending more time with my kids, so I decided to teach them at home.

RADIO PRESENTER: Liz, how do you feel about your mother's decision?

LIZ: Well, my mom and I get along really well, and I think this is essential. We laugh a lot and have fun. As for the work, I go at my own pace. So I can go through lessons as fast or as slowly as I need. That way I don't waste time on easy topics, but I can take more time to go over things that I don't understand immediately. That's just not possible in a normal classroom with 28 or more kids all having their individual strengths and weaknesses. As for the subjects that my mom doesn't teach, like Maths, Spanish and History, we work together with two other families. We meet up four times a week and the other parents teach these subjects, which is a lot of fun, because they are really into their teaching and they know a lot about their subjects.

RADIO PRESENTER: Well, that sounds really good. Nelson, you have carried out several studies on home schooling in the US. What else motivates parents to home school their kids?

NELSON: Today, parents opt for home schooling for a variety of reasons. The majority of homeschoolers say that they want to educate their children according to the family's religious beliefs because sometimes they do not agree with what is taught in public schools. Others are dissatisfied with the local schools and can't, or don't want to, afford the expense of private education. For others it's a way of caring for kids with special needs, like learning disabilities, or of having the freedom and flexibility to travel.

RADIO PRESENTER: It seems that there are a lot of benefits from home schooling. So why are there still so many prejudices against young people who are home schooled?

NELSON: Now, sceptics say that home-schooled children would not be prepared to function normally in society, because they never learned to interact with kids their own age. Sometimes they are also said to be religiously dogmatic. Well, all that depends on the parents' approach to home schooling.

RADIO PRESENTER: Is there any proof of such statements?

NELSON: Various studies have shown that kids who have been home educated do not have more problems to integrate into schools of higher learning than traditional students. And nowadays, even many employers are aware of the positive effects of home schooling because those who have been instructed at home have a reputation for reliability, for taking initiative and for being responsible.

RADIO PRESENTER: Liz, have you ever encountered any prejudices?

LIZ: Well, whenever I meet new people and I tell them that I don't go to a public school but that I'm taught at home, they are sort of surprised that I know how to express myself. A lot of people think we fit the stereotype of unsocialized, sheltered geeks. But, well, my brother, who was also educated at home, just graduated from a state university. He never had any trouble adjusting to college life. But I have to admit that my parents always saw to it that we also had relationships with other children and not only with adults.

RADIO PRESENTER: What a success. But certainly, home schooling is not for everyone. Liz mentioned, for example, that it's essential to have a good relationship with the parents.

SARAH: Yes, that's true. Home schooling doesn't always work as well as with our family. I heard of a girl who was home schooled for four years and she says that not only did she not receive a well-founded education, but the conservative Christian curriculum, according to which she was taught, also had a negative impact on her social skills. So, when she returned to school in her junior year, she had a lot of trouble to catch up with the other kids, because she was way behind schedule. And she had a lot of problems making friends and fitting in. In the end, she graduated two years late and she says that it took her several years to find trust in other adults and overcome her sheltered life she led while being home schooled.

RADIO PRESENTER: Well, as we have seen, this approach to education is not for everybody – but it can be a great option for some. Thanks for being here and talking about your experiences. If you got anything to say about the subject, join our blog on *www.radiotoday.com* and share your opinion with us. Have a nice afternoon.

I   Multiple choice

1.   Home schooling …

   ☒ means that children do not go to public or private schools but are taught by their parents or private tutors.

   ☐ means that parents disapprove of the public and private school system.

   ☐ is not legal in the USA or Great Britain.

2.   Liz is positive about being home schooled because she …

   ☐ has a lot of free time.

   ☒ can learn at her own pace.

   ☐ could not imagine being in a normal classroom.

3.   Sceptics assume that home-schooled children are …

   ☒ not able to integrate into society.

   ☐ educationally ill-prepared.

   ☐ not religiously educated.

4. Home-schooled children …

- [ ] have more problems at schools of higher learning.
- [X] are preferred by employers because of their initiative and sense of responsibility.
- [ ] do not have a reputation for reliability.

II Questions on the text

1. Sarah felt that the education in the public or private school system did not fit her children's needs because it advanced too fast and did not take into consideration their individual strengths and weaknesses. She was also concerned about violence at school and the negative influence that her children's classmates could exert, which might involve alcohol and drug abuse. Apart from that she welcomed the opportunity to spend more time with her children.

2. Some parents attach great importance to the religious education of their children and want to make sure that their children are educated according to their religious beliefs. Other parents opt for home schooling because they are dissatisfied with the local schools or feel that state schools do not care enough for children with special needs. For some it is also important to be flexible as they want to travel with their children.

3. In cases where home schooling was not successful, it failed to provide the children with the required knowledge for them to be able to succeed at schools of higher learning. Another problem is that home-schooled children might not be able to develop sufficient social skills to integrate well.

Notenschlüssel:

1	2	3	4	5	6
16–14	13–12	11–10	9–8	7–5	4–0

15 minutes

I   **Collocations: do, make or take?**   (8 pts)
Have a look at the following words and phrases and decide which of
these verbs is used together with them.

> to do – to make – to take

1. _____ action

2. _____ someone a favour

3. _____ progress

4. _____ a mistake

5. _____ advantage

6. _____ an exam

7. _____ a picture

8. _____ someone harm

II   **Idiomatic collocations**   (10 pts)
Underline the most usual idiomatic collocation in the following
sentences translated from German.

1. *Mein Sohn mag lieber starken Tee.*
   My son prefers **powerful / strong / heavy / intense** tea.

2. *Die Tochter ist ihrer Mutter wie aus dem Gesicht geschnitten.*
   The daughter is the **complete / cutting / spitting / reflecting**
   image of her mother.

3. *Ihr Ehemann sprach Englisch mit einem deutlichen französischen
   Akzent.*
   Her husband spoke English with a(n) **pronounced / explicit /
   wide / considerable** French accent.

4. *Man hat ihn gebeten, ein Referat über seine Arbeit zu halten.*
   He has been asked to **keep / hold / give / commit** a presentation
   about his work.

41

5. *Er ist ein starker Raucher.*
   He is a **strong / hard / big / heavy** smoker.

6. *Meine Mutter ist eine glühende Verehrerin von Shakespeares Werken.*
   My mother is a(n) **glowing / burning / ardent / fiery** admirer of Shakespeare's works.

7. *Als sie von dem Unfall erfuhr, brach sie in Tränen aus.*
   When she heard about the accident, she **burst / blew / collapsed / erupted** into tears.

8. *Meine Schwester hatte schon immer eine lebhafte Fantasie.*
   She has always had a(n) **fresh / bright / vivid / active** imagination.

9. *Sie strengte sich wirklich an, um den Test zu bestehen.*
   She really **made / did / tried / committed** an effort to pass the test.

10. *Das Baby war schon fest eingeschlafen.*
    The baby was already **fast / very / completely / totally** asleep.

III False friends

(8 pts)

Translate the words in brackets so that they fit the sentences.

"Dad, could you please _____ *(bringen)* me to the cinema tomorrow night? And could I possibly _____ *(leihen)* some money? There is a new film that had a very good _____ *(Kritik)* in the newspaper."

"Well, if your _____ *(Noten)* were better, I would probably _____ *(leihen)* you some money to go and watch a film but …"

"Oh, Dad, it'll be in French, so I'll improve my French a lot."

"That's very _____ *(vernünftig)* indeed. Okay, you can go. By the way, how much is a _____ *(Karte)* nowadays?"

"It's about £ 7.50."

"Wow, that's a lot of money. I prefer watching TV on my sofa. What _____ *(Programm)* is that film on later …?"

Solution

I Collocations: do, make or take?

*✎ **Hinweis:** Kollokationen sind Wörter, die häufig gemeinsam auftreten. Ein*
✎ Muttersprachler macht diese Wortkombinationen aus seinem Sprachgefühl
✎ heraus richtig. Für einen Englischlernenden stellen sie jedoch insofern ein
✎ Problem dar, als dass es keine lernbaren Regeln gibt. Berücksichtige beim
✎ Vokabellernen also auch immer die Umgebung, in der ein Wort auftritt und
✎ notiere dir häufige Kollokationen, sodass sie in deinen aktiven Wortschatz
✎ übergehen können.
✎ Wenn du dir bei folgenden do/make/take-*Kollokationen nicht ganz sicher*
✎ bist, wie du sie ins Deutsche übersetzen würdest, schaue im zweisprachigen
✎ Wörterbuch nach.

1. **to take** action
2. **to do** someone a favour
3. **to make** progress
4. **to make** a mistake
5. **to take** advantage
6. **to take** an exam
7. **to take** a picture
8. **to do** someone harm

II Idiomatic collocations

1. *Mein Sohn mag lieber starken Tee.*
   My son prefers **strong** tea.

2. *Die Tochter ist ihrer Mutter wie aus dem Gesicht geschnitten.*
   The daughter is the **spitting** image of her mother.

3. *Ihr Ehemann sprach Englisch mit einem deutlichen französischen Akzent.*
   Her husband spoke English with a **pronounced** French accent.

4. *Man hat ihn gebeten, ein Referat über seine Arbeit zu halten.*
   He has been asked to **give** a presentation about his work.

5. *Er ist ein starker Raucher.*
   He is a **heavy** smoker.

6. *Meine Mutter ist eine glühende Verehrerin von Shakespeares Werken.*
   My mother is an **ardent** admirer of Shakespeare's works.

7. *Als sie von dem Unfall erfuhr, brach sie in Tränen aus.*
   When she heard about the accident, she **burst** into tears.

8. *Meine Schwester hatte schon immer eine lebhafte Phantasie.*
   She has always had a **vivid** imagination.

9. *Sie strengte sich wirklich an, um den Test zu bestehen.*
   She really **made** an effort to pass the test.

10. *Das Baby war schon fest eingeschlafen.*
    The baby was already **fast** asleep.

III False friends

/ ***Hinweis:*** *Nicht nur die idiomatischen Kollokationen stellen Englischlernende*
/ *immer wieder vor Herausforderungen, sondern auch die sogenannten false*
/ *friends, d. h. Wörter die man aufgrund von Ähnlichkeiten mit der Mutter-*
/ *sprache leicht verwechseln kann. Deshalb solltest du sie dir besonders gut*
/ *einprägen und immer in einem geeigneten Kontext lernen.*

"Dad, could you please **take** me to the cinema tomorrow night? And could I possibly **borrow** some money? There is a new film that had a very good **review** in the newspaper."
"Well, if your **grades/marks** were better, I would probably **lend** you some money to go and watch a film but …"
"Oh, Dad, it'll be in French, so I'll improve my French a lot."
"That's very **sensible** indeed. Okay, you can go. By the way, how much is a **ticket** nowadays?"
"It's about £ 7.50."
"Wow, that's a lot of money. I prefer watching TV on my sofa. What **channel** is that film on later …?"

Notenschlüssel:

1	2	3	4	5	6
26–23	22–19	18–16	15–13	12–8	7–0

15 minutes

Taking a gap year – an experience to open your eyes

I   English in use   (20 pts)

Tick the correct form to be used in the sentence from the words given below the text.

Building a school in Kenya, learning about sustainable agriculture in India or dealing _____ (**1**) environmental conservation in Indonesia – there is a wide variety of activities which young people can choose from when they want to take a year off after school.

Sam O'Neil is one of a _____ (**2**) number of young Americans who decided to have a break before going on to college. So after _____ (**3**) high school, he _____ (**4**) one year volunteering in a hospital in Bangladesh and teaching English at an orphanage in Thailand. "The time there was priceless. I learnt so many things and I gained confidence in myself and became much more independent," says Sam, who has just arrived in Princeton to start his first term. "It opened up completely new perspectives."

O'Neil was alone _____ (**5**) his classmates in doing so. Only in the last few years has the idea of taking a year off been gaining popularity in the USA whereas gap years are already quite _____ (**6**) in Europe and Australia. Those young people _____ (**7**) decide not to go on to university immediately but to engage in volunteer work abroad or to _____ (**8**) a working holiday in their home country state that the pressure _____ (**9**) their last high school year has left them exhausted and thus they intend _____ (**10**) burnout. "After all those years of teachers, revision and exams, I felt I was focused on college as a means to an end," explains Sam O'Neil. "So taking some time out after school put my life back into perspective."

45

And that is exactly what guidance counsellors hope for when they encourage students to go abroad before matriculating. They think that students will profit _____ (**11**) a year out of the classroom and achieve personal growth, so that they _____ (**12**) college with a fresh mind and a lot of energy. Nowadays, some of _____ (**13**) top universities even offer financial help in order to enable students from all backgrounds to participate _____ (**14**) a year of volunteer work, _____ (**15**) is considered to be an advantage for their future careers.

When Sam O'Neil planned his year of travel around the globe, he was aware that a gap year had to be more _____ (**16**) rest and leisure to be really beneficial. "I knew that planning a gap year was above all a _____ (**17**) of balancing potential negative and positive aspects. But I had clear goals in my mind: I wanted _____ (**18**) work experience in different fields and I intended to clarify my academic goals," he explains and he adds, "Without _____ (**19**) doubt, this was the best experience of my _____ (**20**)."

1	☐ in	☐ at	☐ with
2	☐ grown	☐ growing	☐ grew
3	☐ finishing	☐ finish	☐ finished
4	☐ spended	☐ has spent	☐ spent
5	☐ among	☐ between	☐ from
6	☐ used	☐ common	☐ general
7	☐ whose	☐ who	☐ which
8	☐ undertake	☐ make	☐ work on
9	☐ while	☐ during	☐ when
10	☐ avoiding	☐ avoid	☐ to avoid
11	☐ from	☐ of	☐ about
12	☐ are starting	☐ start	☐ are going to start
13	☐ Americas	☐ America's	☐ Americas'
14	☐ of	☐ in	☐ at
15	☐ what	☐ that	☐ which

16	☐ then	☐ than	☐ as
17	☐ matter	☐ thing	☐ subject
18	☐ to gain	☐ to earn	☐ to win
19	☐ some	☐ every	☐ any
20	☐ live	☐ life	☐ lives

II Language

Explain what Sam O'Neil says in your own words.

"After all these years of teachers, revision and exams, I felt I was focused on college <u>as a means to an end</u>."

_____

_____

_____

_____

_____

_____

Solution

Taking a gap year – an experience to open your eyes

I   English in use

Hinweis: Bei diesem Aufgabenformat sollst du aus drei möglichen Antworten diejenige auswählen, die im Kontext richtig ist. Hier geht es nicht nur um grammatikalische Kenntnisse (z. B. tenses oder relative pronouns), sondern auch um lexikalische Fragen (z. B. live – life) und manchmal auch um Landeskunde.

#						
1	☐ in	☐ at	☒ with
2	☐ grown	☒ growing	☐ grew
3	☒ finishing	☐ finish	☐ finished
4	☐ spended	☐ has spent	☒ spent
5	☒ among	☐ between	☐ from
6	☐ used	☒ common	☐ general
7	☐ whose	☒ who	☐ which
8	☒ undertake	☐ make	☐ work on
9	☐ while	☒ during	☐ when
10	☐ avoiding	☐ avoid	☒ to avoid
11	☒ from	☐ of	☐ about
12	☐ are starting	☒ start	☐ are going to start
13	☐ Americas	☒ America's	☐ Americas'
14	☐ of	☒ in	☐ at
15	☐ what	☐ that	☒ which
16	☐ then	☒ than	☐ as
17	☒ matter	☐ thing	☐ subject
18	☒ to gain	☐ to earn	☐ to win
19	☐ some	☐ every	☒ any
20	☐ live	☒ life	☐ lives

II Language

Sam O'Neil thinks that he would only put up with college in order to be able to take the next step, such as finding a job and starting a career. He is not interested in college itself.

Notenschlüssel:

1	2	3	4	5	6
22–20	19–17	16–14	13–11	10–7	6–0

20 minutes

Überleben in Australien leicht gemacht

Australien ist ein faszinierender Ort, wo es unter Umständen auch gefährlich werden kann. Hier erfahren Sie alles, was Sie für Reisen durch Australien wissen müssen:

In the Outback

Links fahren!
Fahren Sie auf der linken Straßenseite. Auf langen, geraden Straßen, auf denen einem nur selten ein anderes Auto begegnet, vergisst man als Ausländer oft schnell, dass man in Australien auf der „falschen" Seite fährt. Das kann in einer Kurve fatale Folgen haben. Seien Sie also in Kurven und an Kreuzungen besonders vorsichtig.

Informieren Sie Dritte
Insbesondere wenn Sie vorhaben, auf einsamen Straßen zu reisen, sollten Sie jemandem von Ihren Plänen erzählen. Teilen Sie dieser Person mit, wann Sie voraussichtlich an Ihrem Ziel ankommen werden. So kann jemand einen Suchtrupp losschicken, wenn Sie nicht zur vereinbarten Zeit da sind.

Was tun bei einer Panne?
Verlassen Sie auf keinen Fall das Fahrzeug! Rettungsflugzeuge können ein Auto wesentlich einfacher finden als eine einzelne Person. Suchen Sie sich einen Platz im Schatten und teilen Sie sich das vorhandene Wasser gut ein.

Dehydration / Wassermangel

Nehmen Sie immer genügend Wasser mit und vergessen Sie nicht, es auch zu trinken. Die meisten Todesfälle im Outback sind auf Dehydration, d. h. Wassermangel im Körper zurückzuführen.

On the beach

Sichere Strände

Nach der Tour durch das Outback können Sie sich an einem der wunderschönen Strände entspannen. Am besten bleiben Sie an einem der Strände, die von Rettungsschwimmern überwacht werden. An den roten und gelben Fahnen kann man erkennen, dass hier Rettungsschwimmer bereit stehen und den Strandabschnitt sperren, wenn sie ihn aufgrund von Strömungen, Krokodilen, Quallen oder Haien nicht für sicher halten.

Achtung Kokosnuss!

Setzen Sie sich auf der Suche nach Schatten nicht unter eine Kokospalme. Kokosnüsse sind schwer und fallen oft aus großer Höhe. Jedes Jahr werden weltweit ca. 150 Menschen durch herabfallende Kokosnüsse getötet, zehnmal mehr als von Krokodilen und Haien zusammen. Dies sind alles nur Infos und Tipps, die Ihre Reise sicherer machen sollen. Aber keine Panik! Halten Sie sich an die Grundregeln und Sie werden jede Menge Spaß haben.

Mediation (20 pts)

Imagine you are staying with a host family in Australia for several weeks. Before you left for Australia, you looked for useful information on the Internet. When you came across some interesting "survival tips", you printed them out to take with you.

As your host family is planning a trip to show you parts of the outback, you have a look at the survival tips again. Of course, your host parents also want to know what they say. Answer their questions:

1. Well, what do they say you have to do when travelling through the outback?

2. What about car problems? What are you supposed to do when your car breaks down or when you have a car accident?

3. Dehydration – we have the same word in English. What do they say about that?

4. What does the flag on the beach indicate?

5. Why is there a picture of a coconut tree?

Read through the text thoroughly and choose the information that is necessary to answer the questions. Answer the questions in <u>English</u> and <u>write in complete sentences</u>.

Solution

Überleben in Australien leicht gemacht

Mediation

Hinweis: Bei der Sprachmittlung geht es darum, die gesuchten Informationen zusammenfassend in der Fremdsprache wiederzugeben. Du sollst also nicht Wort für Wort übersetzen, sondern einen Weg finden, mit den dir zur Verfügung stehenden sprachlichen Mitteln das auszudrücken, was erfragt wird.
Achte hier auf die vorgegebene Situation, damit du die wesentlichen Informationen im Text findest und markiere sie. Überlege, wie du Wörter, die du nicht sofort ins Englische übersetzen kannst, umschreiben könntest (z. B. durch eine Paraphrase oder einen allgemeineren Überbegriff). Wenn du z. B. die englischen Worte für „Strömung" und „Qualle" nicht kennst, könntest du in Aufgabe 4 auch schreiben „… because of dangerous animals or water currents".

1. They say that people have to drive on the left-hand side of the road. On long, straight roads, foreigners often forget that in Australia you have to drive on the "wrong" side of the road. So drivers need to be especially careful at junctions and bends.
   If you are travelling on lonely roads, you should tell a third party of your plans and of your estimated time of return. They can then send out a search party if you do not return on time.

2. When your car breaks down, you should stay with your vehicle. Rescue planes can spot a car more easily than a person on their own. You should keep to the shade and not waste your water supply.

3. Dehydration is when there is not enough water in the body. They say that you should always take enough water with you and not forget to drink it because most deaths in the outback are due to dehydration.

4. The red and yellow flags indicate the area of a beach which lifesavers keep an eye on. The lifesavers will close the area if they consider it unsafe because of undertows, jellyfish, crocodiles or sharks.

5. When looking for shade, you should not sit down under a coconut tree because coconuts are heavy and they often fall from great heights. In fact, it says here that every year about 150 people worldwide are killed by falling coconuts.

Notenschlüssel:

1	2	3	4	5	6
20–18	17–15	14–12	11–10	9–6	5–0

20 minutes

Exercise "won't cure child obesity"

Scientists have questioned the assumption[1] that a lack of exercise causes obesity in children.

The study suggests that physical inactivity appears to be the result of obesity, instead of its cause.

5 Researchers said the findings indicate that nutrition[2], rather than exercise, is the best way of tackling[3] childhood obesity.

The EarlyBird[4] team followed more than 200 children in Plymouth over three years, monitoring their fat and exercise levels at regular intervals.

They found that body fat levels had an effect on physical activity, but that vary-
10 ing activity did not lead to any changes in weight.

The paper, published in the Archives of Disease in Childhood[5], suggests that overweight children may think about their body negatively, shying away from sports and exercise as a result.

It concluded: "Physical inactivity appears to be the result of obesity rather than
15 its cause.

"This reverse causality may explain why attempts to tackle childhood obesity by promoting physical activity have been largely unsuccessful."

Dr David Haslam, from the National Obesity Forum, cautioned that the wider health benefits of exercise for children must not be overlooked.

20 He told the BBC: "The EarlyBird team really force us to question our comfort-able assumptions regarding childhood obesity.

"What we, as clinicians must do, is nod reverently[6] at their work, learn lessons from it, and reappraise[7] our own practices accordingly.

"What we shouldn't do is take the paper at face value and allow lean children to
25 be as lazy as they please, as that would be a catastrophic mistake."

A Department of Health spokesman added: "We are committed to tackling child-hood obesity and this study provides some useful messages on the importance of a child's early years and the impact this can have on their future health and be-haviour.

30 "We will consider this evidence alongside other research which has different findings on the link between physical activity and weight when we are develop-ing our policy to produce better public health outcomes."   *(321 words)*

Quelle: http://www.independent.co.uk/life-style/health-and-families/health-news/exercise-wont-cure-child-obesity-2021428.html; Thursday, 8 July 2010.

Annotations

1 assumption – the fact that something is accepted as true without proof or evidence
2 nutrition – food
3 to tackle – to deal with
4 EarlyBird – name of the study
5 Archive of Disease in Childhood – medical journal
6 reverently – with respect
7 to reappraise – to make a new evaluation of sth.

I Working with the text

1. Which question does the text deal with? Form a direct question that expresses the issue. (2 pts)

_____

_____

2. Explain the essential finding of the study in your own words. (2 pts)

_____

_____

_____

_____

3. True, false or not in the text? Tick the correct answer. (6 pts)

		true	false	not in the text
a)	Childhood obesity can be dealt with by changing eating habits.	☐	☐	☐
b)	It has been shown that children with obese parents are more likely to be overweight.	☐	☐	☐
c)	Taking exercise has a great impact on the body fat levels.	☐	☐	☐
d)	The reason why overweight children do not do enough sports is that they cannot accept their body.	☐	☐	☐
e)	Nevertheless, the attempts to make children lose weight by taking regular exercise were successful.	☐	☐	☐
f)	Obese children tend to become overweight adults.	☐	☐	☐

4. Which conclusions does Dr. D. Haslam draw from the findings of the study? (4 pts)

Do:

_____

_____

Don't:

_____

_____

II Cartoon analysis (10 pts)

Describe what you see in the following cartoon and explain why it is funny.

John McPherson / cartoonstock. com

Solution

Exercise "won't cure child obesity"

Hinweis: Hier wird das Textverständnis durch verschiedene Aufgaben abgeprüft. Es ist wichtig, dass du die Aufgabenstellung sorgfältig durchliest. Denke bei true / false /not in the text-*Aufgaben daran, dass hier wirklich nur die Aussagen aus dem Text relevant sind.*

I   Working with the text

1. Does lack of exercise really cause childhood obesity?

2. Until now scientists were of the opinion that those children who did not take any exercise became overweight and obese. But this study now supports the view that it is because of their being overweight that children do not exercise, and not the other way around.

		true	false	not in the text
3. a)	Childhood obesity can be dealt with by changing eating habits.	**X**		
b)	It has been shown that children with obese parents are more likely to be overweight.			**X**
c)	Taking exercise has a great impact on the body fat levels.		**X**	
d)	The reason why overweight children do not do enough sports is that they cannot accept their bodies.	**X**		
e)	Nevertheless, the attempts to make children lose weight by taking regular exercise were successful.		**X**	
f)	Obese children tend to become overweight adults.			**X**

4. **Do:** Respect the findings of the study and reconsider the practices in use.
   Don't: Don't rely completely on the study and don't let children of normal weight become lazy.

57

II Cartoon analysis

In the cartoon, there are two elderly people in their living room. The woman has curly hair and is wearing a flowery dress. She is kneeling next to a man who is probably her husband. He is almost bald and is wearing glasses, checked trousers and a white T-shirt. The man is quite overweight. He is lying flat on his back. On the wall next to him there is a piece of paper reading "Frank's diet progress". On the man's stomach there is a board which the woman uses to draw a line on the wall. There are already several lines on the wall, each with a date next to it. The lines obviously indicate how much weight the man has lost over the years, as he is evidently on a diet.

The funny thing about the cartoon is that you usually mark your children's growth on the wall like that, not someone's waistline.

Notenschlüssel:

1	2	3	4	5	6
24–21	20–18	17–15	14–12	11–8	7–0

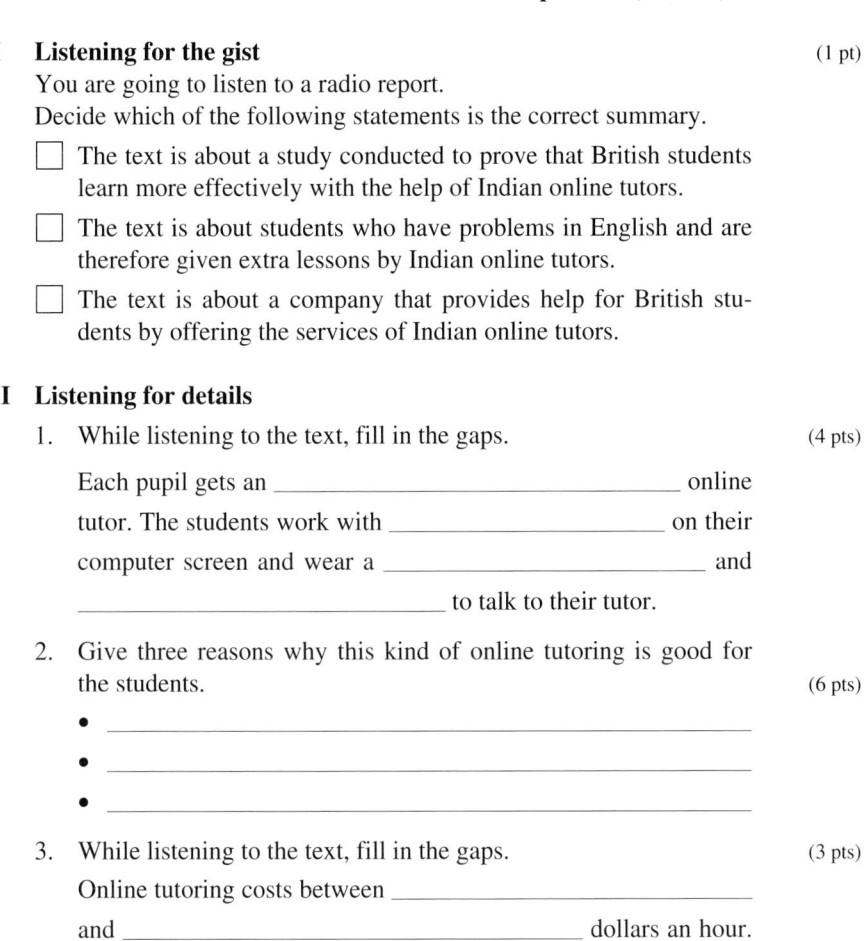

Test 6
Schwerpunkte: *Listening comprehension, vocabulary*

15 minutes

Kids in Britain + online tutors in India = divided opinions (Track 2)

I Listening for the gist   (1 pt)

You are going to listen to a radio report.

Decide which of the following statements is the correct summary.

☐ The text is about a study conducted to prove that British students learn more effectively with the help of Indian online tutors.

☐ The text is about students who have problems in English and are therefore given extra lessons by Indian online tutors.

☐ The text is about a company that provides help for British students by offering the services of Indian online tutors.

II Listening for details

1. While listening to the text, fill in the gaps.   (4 pts)

   Each pupil gets an _____ online

   tutor. The students work with _____ on their

   computer screen and wear a _____ and

   _____ to talk to their tutor.

2. Give three reasons why this kind of online tutoring is good for the students.   (6 pts)

   • _____

   • _____

   • _____

3. While listening to the text, fill in the gaps.   (3 pts)

   Online tutoring costs between _____

   and _____ dollars an hour.

   An online tutor is about _____

   of traditional face-to-face coaching.

59

4. Give the reason why the National Union of Teachers does not approve of this kind of online tutoring. (2 pts)

_____

_____

II Language (4 pts)
Explain the expression "outsourcing of tutors".

_____

_____

_____

_____

_____

_____

_____

_____

Solution

Kids in Britain + online tutors in India = divided opinions (Tapescript)

This is the VOA Special English Education Report.

India was once a colony in the British Empire. But now Indian tutors are helping to teach math to some British children over high-speed Internet connections.

Early results suggest that online tutoring may improve student performance. But not everyone is happy at this so-called outsourcing of tutors.

(SOUND)

It's three-thirty in the afternoon at Raynham Primary School in London. Students are gathering for their after-school math lesson.

Five time zones and thousands of kilometers away, their math tutors are also arriving for class.

(SOUND)

Each pupil gets an individual online tutor. The students work with activities on their computer screen and wear a headset and microphone to talk to their tutor.

Their classroom teacher, Altus Basson, says he has seen an improvement in results.

ALTUS BASSON: "Children who struggle to focus in class focus a lot more or better on the laptops."

Nine-year-old Samia Abdul-Kadir says she enjoys the online lessons.

SAMIA ABDUL-KADIR: "It helps me and, er … because sometimes when we're doing it in class, I don't hear the teacher very much and I don't understand, but online is better."

Her friend, Abdul-Fadil Badori, agrees.

ABDUL-FADIL BADORI: "Online, you can hear it, cause it's not shared by everyone, everyone has different topics they're learning."

Tom Hooper started the company that provides the online tutoring: BrightSpark Education.

TOM HOOPER: "Children today feel very confident online, they feel very engaged, they feel very in control. And that's half the battle with education. Give them control, make them feel confident and enjoy their learning and there you'll see them start to improve and embrace it."

Online tutoring costs between twenty and twenty-five dollars an hour. An online tutor is about half the cost of traditional face-to-face coaching.

But some people say an Internet connection is not enough of a connection for teaching and learning. Kevin Courtney is deputy general secretary of Britain's National Union of Teachers.

KEVIN COURTNEY: "We think that there's something that's a really important emotional connection between a teacher and a child, whether it's a whole class or whether it's one-to-one, that you need that immediacy of feedback, and we're not convinced that that can happen across an Internet connection. In one of the wealthiest countries in the world, we think that we can afford to have teachers with the genuine emotional connection there with the children."

BrightSpark Education says the online tutoring is used only as an addition to supplement regular teaching. The company says its service does not represent a threat to teachers' jobs in Britain.

Some parents say they are satisfied with the results. And what about the children?

CHILDREN: "I love it!" "I love it!" "I hate maths!"

So math – or, as the British call it, maths – is still not everyone's favorite subject even with the latest technology to teach it.

And that's the VOA Special English Education Report. You can watch a video of the online tutoring by going to voaspecialenglish.com. I'm Steve Ember.

VOA Voice of America, http://www.voanews.com/learningenglish/home/education/British-Kids--Online-Tutors-in-India--Divided-Opinions-120320714.html

I Listening for the gist

☐ The text is about a study conducted to prove that British students learn more effectively with the help of Indian online tutors.

☐ The text is about students who have problems in English and are therefore given extra lessons by Indian online tutors.

☒ The text is about a company that provides help for British students by offering the services of Indian online tutors.

II Listening for details

1. Each pupil gets an **individual** online tutor. The students work with **activities** on their computer screen and wear a **headset** and **microphone** to talk to their tutor.

2. • Students who are not able to concentrate on the subject in class focus better on the computer.
   • Students sometimes cannot hear the teacher well and so do not understand.
   • Every student can work on the topic that is a problem for him/her.
   • The students are in control and very confident and this improves learning.

3. Online tutoring costs between **twenty** and **twenty-five** dollars an hour. An online tutor is about **half the cost** of traditional face-to-face coaching.

4. The important emotional connection between teacher and student is lacking.

III Language

"Outsourcing" is a term used in business. It means that a certain business process (e. g. parts of the production or financial management) is not done within the company but transferred to an external service provider. This often involves the business processes concerned being transferred abroad because labour is cheaper there.

In the context of the text, "outsourcing of tutors" means that the students are not taught by British teachers, but by tutors who are in India working via the Internet. And as it is stated in the text, this practice is much cheaper than traditional, local coaching.

Notenschlüssel:

1	2	3	4	5	6
20–18	17–15	14–12	11–10	9–6	5–0

15 minutes

Mixed bag   (20 pts)

Complete the text by

(**1**) putting the verb in brackets in the correct tense and form required,

(**2**) replacing the participle construction with a different construction,

(**3**) replacing the given construction with a different construction without changing the rest of the sentence.

(**4**) replacing the active sentence with a passive one.

Cyber bullying

Every one of us _____ (to have) (**1**) some sort of experience with bullies in our lives. There have always been children _____ (picking) (**2**) on other children, usually on those unable or too afraid to fight back and defend themselves. In the last thirty years, however, new means of communication _____ _____ (to open up) (**1**) new possibilities for bullies not content with making their victims _____ (to suffer) (**1**) during school hours. Nowadays, they _____ (to call) (**1**) "cyber bullies" and they use social networks and text messages to harass, humiliate or threaten their victims at any time, even at night or at weekends.

_____ (to send) (**1**) nasty text messages or _____ (to post) (**1**) defamatory notes on social networks and other websites are rather straightforward acts of cyber bullying. But _____ (they also use other, less obvious methods) (**4**): Cyber bullies _____ (who pretend) (**3**) to be another person online might leave unflattering messages or they might give away personal information about their victim. With the help of built-in digital cameras in mobile phones, pictures or videos _____ _____ (showing) (**2**) another child in an embarrassing situation can now be widely distributed within seconds without the child knowing about it. _____ _____ (Only the bullies' imagination and their access to technology limit the methods used) (**4**).

In fact, cyber bullying can be much worse than face-to-face bullying; although there is no physical violence involved, cyber bullying is extremely terrifying since it is merciless and public – potentially everybody on the Internet can observe and witness what is going on – and at the same time anonymous as there seems to be nobody _____ (caring) (**2**) to interfere and stop the abuse. Actually most of the children who fall victim to cyber bullying never report it. But some of them are seriously affected after _____ (they have been involved) (**3**) in a cyber bullying incident. There are even cases where children have committed suicide or killed each other.

_____ (With their victims not being present) (**3**), cyber bullies are not immediately confronted with their victims' distress and suffering, which minimises any feelings of regret or compassion towards them. And the anonymity of the Internet has not only offered a new platform for those who _____ (already, to make) (**1**) an appearance as playground bullies, but it has also given the shy and quiet children who would never have thought of bullying others in person the power to do so in the virtual world.

What can children do when _____ (cyber bullies target them) (**4**)? The best way to avoid being cyber bullied is prevention. Children should be told never to give out any personal information or passwords and not to believe everything they see or read on the Internet. When _____ (finding) (**2**) a mean or defamatory message, they should not reply, but get help from adults or even the police.

Solution

Mixed bag

Hinweis: Bei dieser Aufgabe sollst du zeigen, dass du weißt, wie Partizipialkonstruktionen beispielsweise in Relativsätze oder Kausalsätze aufgelöst werden oder
umgekehrt bestimmte Strukturen durch Partizipialkonstruktionen ersetzt werden
können.
Auch die Zeitformen und die Umformung von Aktiv- in Passivsätze solltest du be-
herrschen. Wenn du dir hier nicht mehr ganz sicher bist, schlage noch einmal in
der Kurzgrammatik am Anfang dieses Buches nach.

Cyber bullying

Every one of us **has had** some sort of experience with bullies in our lives. There
have always been children **who pick** on other children, usually on those unable or
too afraid to fight back and defend themselves. In the last thirty years, however, new
means of communication **have opened up** new possibilities for bullies not content
with making their victims **suffer** during school hours. Nowadays, they **are called**
"cyber bullies" and they use social networks and text messages to harass, humiliate
or threaten their victims at any time, even at night or at weekends.
Sending nasty text messages or **posting** defamatory notes on social networks and
other websites are rather straightforward acts of cyber bullying. But **other, less
obvious methods are also used**: Cyber bullies **pretending** to be another person online might leave unflattering messages or they might give away personal information
about their victim. With the help of built-in digital cameras in mobile phones, pictures or videos **that/which show** another child in an embarrassing situation can now
be widely distributed within seconds without the child knowing about it. **The
methods used are limited only by the bullies' imagination and their access to
technology**.
In fact, cyber bullying can be much worse than face-to-face bullying; although there
is no physical violence involved, cyber bullying is extremely terrifying since it is
merciless and public – potentially everybody on the Internet can observe and witness
what is going on – and at the same time anonymous as there seems to be nobody
who cares to interfere and stop the abuse. Actually most of the children who fall
victim to cyber bullying never report it. But some of them are seriously affected
after **having been involved** in a cyber bullying incident. There are even cases where
children have committed suicide or killed each other.
**As/Since/Because their victims are not present/Without their victims being
present**, cyber bullies are not immediately confronted with their victims' distress
and suffering, which minimises any feelings of regret or compassion towards them.
And the anonymity of the Internet has not only offered a new platform for those who
have already made an appearance as playground bullies, but it has also given the

66

shy and quiet children who would never have thought of bullying others in person the power to do so in the virtual world.

What can children do when **they are targeted by cyber bullies**? The best way to avoid being cyber bullied is prevention. Children should be told never to give out any personal information or passwords and not to believe everything they see or read on the Internet. When **they find** a mean or defamatory message, they should not reply, but get help from adults or even the police.

Notenschlüssel:

1	2	3	4	5	6
20–18	17–15	14–12	11–10	9–7	6–0

15 minutes

Spot the mistake (20 pts)

Read the text. Then decide whether the underlined words are correct English or not. If not, write your corrections on the lines on the right.

The British and their monarchy

Although it <u>was</u> predicted for years (especially in the aftermath of Princess <u>Dianas</u> death) that the British monarchy would <u>inevitably</u> come to an end because it was outdated and unnecessary, the Royals still <u>hold</u> a certain fascination, not only for the British but for a lot of people. That cannot be denied. On the <u>marriage</u> day of Prince William and Princess Catherine, thousands of spectators lined the <u>roads</u> and millions more followed the pageantry in front of TV screens all over the world. <u>Given</u> the recent history of royal marriages (or rather divorces), it seems that this wedding will help to revive the monarchy and boost opinion <u>poles</u>: These show that the vast majority of the British still favour <u>keeping</u> things the way they are.

For the <u>supporters</u> of the monarchy, it is something extraordinary to be represented by a queen or a king. There are only a few big monarchies left, with the British monarchy currently <u>been the</u> longest lasting monarchy in the world. So, for the British, the monarchy means stability. In addition to that, royalty is at the heart of the British national <u>proud</u>. It gives them a centre and the possibility <u>to identify</u> with their Royal Family as well as with their country. The British monarchy embodies British history and identity.

Furthermore, the monarchy creates its own <u>celebrities</u>. Not only <u>do</u> the members of the Royal Family belong to the nobility, but they are also very attractive to the media, <u>regular</u> hitting the headlines of <u>tabloid</u> newspapers and boosting sales figures. Many people see the Royals as role models, just as actors or singers are role models for others.

So, if the British monarchy <u>would really be</u> abolished, ———————————
the British and the whole world would certainly <u>loose</u> ———————————
a source of fascination and also inspiration. Who <u>has</u> ———————————
<u>never dreamt</u> of becoming a princess or a prince? ———————————
Without royalty these dreams would become impos-
sible; and that would be a pity.

Solution

Spot the mistake

Hinweis: Hier sollst du einmal in die Rolle einer Lehrkraft schlüpfen und Fehler korrigieren. Freundlicherweise sind die möglichen Fehler schon unterstrichen. Aber Achtung: Nicht alle unterstrichenen Wörter sind auch falsch. Fehler können sich auf Grammatik (z. B. Zeitengebrauch), Wortschatz oder Orthographie beziehen.

The British and their monarchy

Although it ~~was~~ predicted for years (especially in the	has been
aftermath of Princess ~~Dianas~~ death) that the British	Diana's
monarchy would inevitably come to an end because it	
was outdated and unnecessary, the Royals still hold a	
certain fascination, not only for the British but for a lot	
of people. That cannot be denied. On the ~~marriage~~ day	wedding
of Prince William and Princess Catherine, thousands	
of spectators lined the ~~roads~~ and millions more	streets
followed the pageantry in front of TV screens all over	
the world. Given the recent history of royal marriages	
(or rather divorces), it seems that this wedding will	
help to revive the monarchy and boost opinion ~~poles~~:	polls
These show that the vast majority of the British still	
favour keeping things the way they are.	
For the supporters of the monarchy, it is something	
extraordinary to be represented by a queen or a king.	
There are only a few big monarchies left, with the Brit-	
ish monarchy currently ~~been~~ the longest lasting mon-	being
archy in the world. So, for the British, the monarchy	
means stability. In addition to that, royalty is at the	
heart of the British national ~~proud~~. It gives them a	pride
centre and the possibility ~~to identify~~ with their Royal	of identifying
Family as well as with their country. The British mon-	
archy embodies British history and identity.	
Furthermore, the monarchy creates its own celebrities.	
Not only do the members of the Royal Family belong	
to the nobility, but they are also very attractive to the	
media, ~~regular~~ hitting the headlines of tabloid news-	regularly
papers and boosting sales figures. Many people see the	
Royals as role models, just as actors or singers are role	
models for others.	

So, if the British monarchy ~~would really be~~ abolished,   _were/was really_
the British and the whole world would certainly ~~loose~~   _lose_
a source of fascination and also inspiration. Who <u>has</u>
<u>never dreamt</u> of becoming a princess or a prince?
Without royalty these dreams would become impossible; and that would be a pity.

Notenschlüssel:

1	2	3	4	5	6
20–18	17–15	14–12	11–10	9–6	5–0

20 minutes

I Vocabulary: Types of crime (8 pts)

Fill in the missing words in the table.

Crime	Criminal	Verb
		to set fire to sth.
assault		
	blackmailer	
burglary		
		to kidnap s.o
murder		
	robber	
		to steal sth.

II Vocabulary: Motives for crime (9 pts)

Translate the German words and phrases into English and complete the text.

People _____ (*Verbrechen begehen*) for various reasons. The main reason is _____ (*Armut*). Sometimes emotions, such as love and _____ (*Eifersucht*), play an important role and people act on impulse, _____ (*spontan*), without thinking of the consequences.

Many people _____ (*verhaftet werden*) for crimes they committed while _____ (*unter Drogen- und Alkoholeinfluss*).

A lot of criminal acts are also motivated by _____ (*Gier*) and the desire to get rich quickly. One crime might also lead to an other, e. g. if the first crime _____ (wurde beobachtet) by someone and the _____ (Straftäter*in) intends to protect his/her secret.

III Vocabulary: Cybercrime
(5 pts)
Write the clues for the following words.

```
                    2
                    C
                    Y
                    B
                    E
          1         R
          H    3    P  H  I  S  H  I  N  G
          A         I
     4    C  Y  B  E  R  S  T  A  L  K  I  N  G
          K         A
          I         C
   5  I D E  N  T  I  T  Y     T  H  E  F  T
          G
```

Down:

1 _____

_____

2 _____

_____

Across:

3 _____

_____

4 _____

_____

5 _____

_____

73

Solution

Hinweis: Es ist wichtig, dass du die Vokabeln, die du lernst, so vielfältig wie möglich vernetzt. Bei der vorliegenden Tabelle geht es darum, nicht nur die Verben, sondern auch die entsprechenden Substantive zu kennen. Diese lassen sich nicht immer voneinander ableiten.

I   Vocabulary: Types of crime

Crime	Criminal	Verb
arson	**arsonist**	to set fire to sth.
assault	**attacker**	**to assault s.o.**
blackmail	blackmailer	**to blackmail s.o.**
burglary	**burglar**	**to burgle s.th.**
kidnapping	**kidnapper**	to kidnap s.o
murder	**murderer**	**to murder s.o.** **to kill s.o.**
robbery	robber	**to rob s.o. / sth**
theft	**thief**	to steal sth.

II   Vocabulary: Motives for crime

People **commit crimes** for various reasons. The main reason is **poverty**. Sometimes emotions, such as love and **jealousy**, play an important role and people act on impulse, **on the spur of the moment/spontaneously**, without thinking of the consequences.

Many people **are arrested** for crimes they committed while **under the influence of drugs and alcohol**.

A lot of criminal acts are also motivated by **greed** and the desire to get rich quickly. One crime might also lead to another, e. g. if the first crime **was witnessed** by someone and the **perpetrator/offender/criminal** intends to protect his/her secret.

III Vocabulary: Cybercrime

Hinweis: Hier geht es darum, dass du die im Kreuzworträtsel vorgegebenen Wörter erklärst. Wenn du bestimmte Fachbegriffe aus dem Kontext des Wortes nicht kennst, solltest du sie umschreiben. So könntest du z. B. bei der Erklärung für „phishing" (Across – 3) auch „fake" statt „forged" schreiben oder „to get" statt „to elicit".

Down:

1   breaking into a computer system without permission in order to find or destroy information

2   the crime of illegally copying copyrighted material from the Internet, such as music, books, films etc.

Across:

3   the use of forged e-mails or websites in order to elicit personal information from someone

4   the use of the Internet to harass, intimidate or threaten someone repeatedly

5   a crime involving the illegal use of someone else's personal information, such as their bank details or their passport number

Notenschlüssel:

1	2	3	4	5	6
22–20	19–17	16–14	13–11	10–7	6–0

15 minutes

Mixed tenses

Put the verbs in parentheses in the correct tense. Use the passive voice where necessary.

James Bond – crime does pay   (34 pts)

James Bond _____ (to walk) across the screen, perceived by the audience through the barrel of a gun. It is not known who _____ (to point) the gun at him. All of a sudden, realising that he is about to be killed, Bond _____ (to turn around) and _____ (to shoot) directly at the gun and the unknown assailant's blood _____ (to spill) down the screen.

Anyone who _____ (ever, to see) a James Bond film _____ (to know) this part of the famous opening scenes of one of the longest running film series to date. When Ian Fleming (1908–1964) _____ (to publish) his first James Bond novel with the title *Casino Royale* in 1953, he certainly _____ (not to know) that this _____ (to make) him the most successful British crime writer of all time.

Altogether Fleming _____ (to write) twelve novels and nine short stories about the British spy. So far his books _____ *(to sell)* over 100 million copies. But it _____ (to be) the series of Bond films that really _____ (to make) him rich. *Dr. No*, the first film about the famous MI6 agent with the licence to kill, _____ (to produce) in 1962. Since then 24 films _____ (to release). The early films _____ (to base on) Fleming's novels, then original storylines _____ (to write) for the subsequent films. So far, the character of the famous spy

_____ (to play) by various actors, such as Sean Connery and Roger Moore, and each of them _____ (to interpret) the role differently.

When Pierce Brosnan _____ (to take over) as 007 in the film *GoldenEye* in 1995, the first film of the series which _____ (to produce) after the collapse of the Soviet Union, many critics _____ (to doubt) whether Bond still _____ (to matter) in a modern world because many of the previous films _____ (to rely on) the Cold War as the background for the plot. Nonetheless, *GoldenEye* _____ (to be), at that date, the most successful film of the series financially. So, Brosnan _____ (to star) in three more films.

The actor currently playing the role _____ (to be) Daniel Craig, who _____ (to hire) in 2005. Although he _____ (to have to) face a lot of criticism at the beginning, his first appearance in *Casino Royale* (actually Fleming's first Bond novel) _____ (to be) a great success. Craig's second film – the 22nd Bond film – with the title *Quantum of Solace* _____ (to release) in 2008, followed by several more. The most recent film is *No Time to Die*. This certainly _____ (not, to be) the last film of the 007 series, since the world _____ (to have to) be saved in the future, too.

Solution

Mixed tenses

✏ *Hinweis: Setze die Verben in der korrekten Form ein. Denke dabei an die Signal-*
✏ *wörter (z. B. so far, in 1995); sie können dir helfen die richtige Zeitform zu finden.*
✏ *Achte außerdem auf den Sinn der Sätze, damit du wo nötig Passivformen einsetzt.*

James Bond – crime does pay

James Bond **walks/is walking** across the screen, perceived by the audience through the barrel of a gun. It is not known who **is pointing** the gun at him. All of a sudden, realising that he is about to be killed, Bond **turns around** and **shoots** directly at the gun and the unknown assailant's blood **spills** down the screen.

Anyone who **has ever seen** a James Bond film **knows** this part of the famous opening scenes of one of the longest running film series to date. When Ian Fleming (1908–1964) **published** his first James Bond novel with the title *Casino Royale* in 1953, he certainly **did not know** that this **would make** him the most successful British crime writer of all time.

Altogether Fleming **wrote** twelve novels and nine short stories about the British spy. So far his books **have sold** over 100 million copies. But it **was** the series of Bond films that really **made** him rich. *Dr. No*, the first film about the famous MI6 agent with the licence to kill, **was produced** in 1962. Since then 24 films **have been released**. The early films **were based on** Fleming's novels, then original storylines **were written** for the subsequent films. So far, the character of the famous spy **has been played** by various actors, such as Sean Connery and Roger Moore, and each of them **has interpreted** the role differently.

When Pierce Brosnan **took over** as 007 in the film *GoldenEye* in 1995, the first film of the series which **was produced** after the collapse of the Soviet Union, many critics **doubted** whether Bond still **mattered** in a modern world because many of the previous films **had relied on** the Cold War as the background for the plot. Nonetheless, *GoldenEye* **was**, at that date, the most successful film of the series financially. So, Brosnan **starred** in three more films.

The actor currently playing the role **is** Daniel Craig, who **was hired** in 2005. Although he **had to** face a lot of criticism at the beginning, his first appearance in *Casino Royale* (actually Fleming's first Bond novel) **was** a great success. Craig's second film – the 22nd Bond film – with the title *Quantum of Solace* **was released** in 2008, followed by several more. The most recent film is *No Time to Die*. This certainly **will not/won't be** the last film of the 007 series, since the world **will have to** be saved in the future, too.

Notenschlüssel:

1	2	3	4	5	6
34–30	29–25	24–21	20–17	16–11	10–0

25 minutes

'Global war on drugs has failed,' key panel[1] says

Commission criticizes US approach and argues that governments should end the criminalization of drug use

NEW YORK – The global war on drugs has failed and governments should explore legalizing marijuana and other controlled substances, according to a commission that includes former heads of state, a former U.N. secretary-general and a business mogul[2]. A new report by the Global Commission on Drug Policy
5 argues that the decades-old worldwide "war on drugs has failed, with devastating consequences for individuals and societies around the world." [...]
"Political leaders and public figures should have the courage to articulate publicly what many of them acknowledge privately: that the evidence overwhelmingly[3] demonstrates that repressive strategies will not solve the drug problem,
10 and that the war on drugs has not, and cannot, be won," the report said.
[...]
"The United States should look at the extraordinary costs that the policies it has pursued have brought about," said Sir Keith Morris, who is on the advisory board[4] of the International Council on Security and Development, a think tank[5]
15 that seeks to reform drug policies.
"It should look at the huge costs of incarcerating large numbers of people, the damage it's done ... (and) the extraordinary situation with armed conflicts and militant groups – financed by consumption in the U.S. and U.K. – killing British and American troops."
20 Instead of punishing users who the report says "do no harm to others," the commission argues that governments should end criminalization of drug use, experiment with legal models that would undermine organized crime syndicates and offer health and treatment services for drug-users in need.
"Vast expenditures[6] on criminalization and repressive measures directed at pro-
25 ducers, traffickers[7] and consumers of illegal drugs have clearly failed to effectively curtail supply or consumption," the report added. "Apparent victories in eliminating one source or trafficking organization are negated almost instantly by the emergence of other sources and traffickers."
The commission called for drug policies based on methods empirically proven
30 to reduce crime, lead to better health and promote economic and social development.

"Arresting and incarcerating tens of millions of these people in recent decades has filled prisons and destroyed lives and families without reducing the availability of illicit drugs or the power of criminal organizations," the report said.
35 "There appears to be almost no limit to the number of people willing to engage in such activities to better their lives, provide for their families, or otherwise escape poverty. Drug control resources are better directed elsewhere."

'Alternatives'

The commission is especially critical of the United States, saying it must change
40 its antidrug policies from being guided by anti-crime approaches to ones rooted in healthcare and human rights.
"We hope this country (the U.S.) at least starts to think there are alternatives," former Colombian president Gaviria told The Associated Press by phone. "We don't see the U.S. evolving in a way that is compatible with our (countries')
45 long-term interests."
The office of White House drug czar Gil Kerlikowske said the report was misguided[8].
"Drug addiction is a disease that can be successfully prevented and treated. Making drugs more available – as this report suggests – will make it harder to
50 keep our communities healthy and safe," Office of National Drug Control Policy spokesman Rafael Lemaitre said.
[…]

(519 words)

© *AP/dapd*

Annotations
1   key panel – group of experts
2   mogul – an important and powerful person
3   overwhelmingly – very strongly
4   advisory board – a group of individuals who have been selected to make suggestions about what should be done
5   think tank – a group of people organized for intensive research and solving of problems
6   expenditure – the amount of money spent on sth.
7   trafficker – a person who buys and sells drugs
8   misguided – based on error; mistaken

I   Synonyms   (3 pts)

Give synonyms for the underlined words taken from the text.

1. "incarcerating large numbers of people" (l. 16)

_____

2. "failed to effectively curtail supply or consumption" (ll. 25/26)

_____

3. "without reducing the availability of illicit drugs" (ll. 33/34)

_____

II   Language   (4 pts)

Explain the following words taken from the text in your own words.

1. to negate (l. 27)

_____

_____

2. approach (l. 40)

_____

_____

III   True, false or not in the text

Tick the correct answer.
If the statement is false, correct it.

	true	false	not in the text	(8 pts)
1. According to the Global Commission on Drug Policy the global war on drugs has been lost.	☐	☐	☐	
_____				
2. The commission suggests that drug trafficking be legalised.	☐	☐	☐	
_____				
3. Politicians and celebrities should announce publicly that drug abuse is dangerous.	☐	☐	☐	
_____				
_____				

		true	false	not in the text
4.	The United States has spent more money on its drug policies than on its health care system.	☐	☐	☐

_____

_____

| 5. | The experts think that more money should be spent on reforming drug policies. | ☐ | ☐ | ☐ |

_____

_____

| 6. | The policies pursued so far are responsible for armed conflicts in which British and American people die. | ☐ | ☐ | ☐ |

_____

_____

IV Questions on the text   (5 pts)

Answer the following questions using your own words as far as is appropriate. Write one or two sentences only.

1. Why do people get involved in drug dealing?

_____

_____

_____

_____

2. Why did the report meet with criticism?

_____

_____

_____

_____

82

Solution

'Global war on drugs has failed,' key panel says

Hinweis: Dieser Test besteht neben den bekannten „questions on the text", die hier um eine true/false/not in the text-Aufgabe ergänzt sind, aus einem Teil, der explizit Wortschatzkenntnisse abprüft. Lies dir den Kontext der angegebenen Wörter durch. Er ist wichtig, um die entsprechenden Synonyme (d. h. ein Wort mit derselben Bedeutung) zu finden bzw. ein Wort erklären zu können.

I Synonyms

1. putting in prison/imprisoning
2. reduce/decrease
3. illegal

II Language

1. to make/render ineffective
2. a way of dealing with something

III True, false or not in the text

		true	false	not in the text
1.	According to the Global Commission on Drug Policy the global war on drugs has been lost.	☒	☐	☐
2.	The commission suggests that **drugs (marijuana and other controlled substances) be legalised, not drug trafficking.**	☐	☒	☐
3.	Politicians and celebrities should announce publicly that **repressive actions will not solve the drug problem.**	☐	☒	☐
4.	The United States has spent more money on its drug policies than on its health care system.	☐	☐	☒
5.	The experts think that more money should be spent on reforming drug policies.	☐	☐	☒
6.	The policies pursued so far are responsible for armed conflicts in which British and American people die.	☒	☐	☐

IV Questions on the text

1. A lot of people get involved in drug dealing because they want to take care of their families, to have a better life or to get rich quickly.

2. A spokesman from the Office of National Drug Control Policy stated that the report was based on an error because making drugs more easily accessible to everybody is likely to make it more difficult to prevent crime and safeguard people's health.

Notenschlüssel:

1	2	3	4	5	6
20–18	17–15	14–12	11–10	9–6	5–0

15 minutes

Red Nose Day (Track 3)

Listening for details

1. While listening to the text, fill in the gaps. (10 pts)

   Comic Relief is a _____ _____
   based in the UK and it was launched from a _____
   _____ in Sudan on _____ _____ in
   1985 live on TV. Now at that time, there was a devastating
   _____ which was crippling _____ and
   Comic Relief was set up to _____ _____ for that.

2. Answer the following questions in complete sentences. (12 pts)

   a) Why is the charity organisation called Comic Relief?

   _____

   _____

   _____

   _____

   b) What happens on Red Nose Day?

   _____

   _____

   _____

   _____

   c) When was the first Red Nose Day and how much money has
      been raised so far?

   _____

   _____

   _____

   _____

d) What happens with the money?

_____

_____

_____

_____

3. Name four of the things that people do to raise money on Red Nose Day.

(4 pts)

- _____
- _____
- _____
- _____

Solution

Red Nose Day (Tapescript)

JACKIE: Every year in March, celebrities and the general public join together for Red Nose Day.

RICHARD: Yes, you'll see people wearing red noses, red noses on cars, red noses on shirts, the UK is awash with red noses. So for this week's podcastsinenglish.com we're talking about Red Nose Day and finding out what it's all about.

JACKIE: Well, it all started with Comic Relief back in 1985.

RICHARD: Yes. Comic Relief er … is a major charity er … based in the UK and it was launched um … from a refugee camp in Sudan on Christmas Day in 1985 live on TV. Now at that time er … there was a devastating famine which was crippling Ethiopia and Comic Relief was set up to raise money for that.

JACKIE: Yes, and the reason it's called Comic Relief is because it's about getting British comedians to make the public laugh while they raise money to help people.

RICHARD: Yes. Now where does Red Nose Day come in?

JACKIE: Well, Comic Relief is … is the charity, and that works 365 days every year. But every odd year*, so this year 2011, there's a special day – Red Nose Day. It's a huge event on live TV which brings together comedy and charity. People watch the show and donate money. The first Red Nose Day in 1988 raised 15 million pounds.

RICHARD: Yes. And eleven more Red Nose Days have followed um … raising a total of 459 million pounds.

JACKIE: So where does the money go? Well it goes to support people and communities in the UK and in Africa.

RICHARD: So, what's happening this year?

JACKIE: Well, if you go onto the website um … there's loads of information. It's full of fundraising ideas and it tells you what celebrities have already been doing to make people laugh and make money. But there's lots of ideas about how the public … the general public can get involved as well.

RICHARD: Yes, my sister's getting involved. She's actually wearing a pair of pyjamas for the entire day so she's going to be wandering round the street in pyjamas.

JACKIE: And … and so how does that help, wearing the pyjamas, Richard?

RICHARD: Well, she's going to be raising money for that. She's getting people to sponsor her.

JACKIE: Mmm, but some people, they eat something funny or, you know, they make some special food which they sell or they … they do something funny with their hair or wear a red wig. There's lots of different things.

RICHARD: And of course everybody is buying red noses and T-shirts, as we've said.

© *podcastsinenglish.com*

Annotation

* This should say "every other year"

87

Listening for details

1. Comic Relief is a **major charity** based in the UK and it was launched from a **refugee camp** in Sudan on **Christmas Day** in 1985 live on TV. Now at that time, there was a devastating **famine** which was crippling **Ethiopia** and Comic Relief was set up to **raise money** for that.

2. a) The charity organisation is called Comic Relief because British comedians raise money by making the public laugh.

   b) On Red Nose Day, there is a live TV show with a lot of comedy. While watching the show, people give money to the charity organisation.

   c) The first Red Nose Day was in 1988. Since then, 459 million pounds have been raised.

   d) People and communities in the UK and in Africa are supported with the money.

3. • wearing pyjamas all day
   • eating something funny
   • selling special, home-made food
   • doing something funny with their hair
   • wearing a red wig
   • buying red noses and T-shirts

Notenschlüssel:

1	2	3	4	5	6
26–23	22–19	18–16	15–13	12–8	7–0

15 minutes

I   Synonyms, opposites and word families   (17 pts)
Find synonyms, opposites or words from the same word family for
the following words. Sometimes you can find more than one word.

1. **courage**
   adjective: _____

   verb: _____

   opposite of verb: _____

2. **to grow**
   noun: _____

   adjective: _____

   synonym of verb: _____

3. **obedience**
   verb: _____

   adjective: _____

   opposite of noun: _____

4. **memorable**
   noun: _____

   verb: _____

5. **offence**
   verb: _____

   adjective: _____

   noun: _____

6. **to respond**
   noun: _____

   opposite of verb: _____

   synonym of verb: _____

II Phrasal and prepositional verbs   (7 pts)

Fill in the blanks using the words below.

down – into – off – out – up

Three weeks ago, I asked _____ that girl from my class. Her name is Angela and she is really beautiful. And, believe it or not, she did not turn me _____, but she actually showed _____ for our date. And she looked gorgeous. The T-shirt she was wearing really brought _____ the colour of her eyes …

Well, we went to an amusement park and had a great time together. We really hit it _____. I even took some pictures. First I was afraid that there wasn't enough light, but they actually turned _____ great.

After that first date, we agreed to go out again. But I didn't dare to ring her _____. Well, if you want to tell me _____ and say that I am an idiot, you are right. Last Wednesday, I ran _____ her in the grocer's shop and the situation was completely embarrassing. Nevertheless, we talked for a while and it turned _____ that she was really depressed because she had not done well in her last exams. So I decided not to miss _____ on the chance to cheer her _____ and I told her that I wanted to take her _____ to the cinema.

Today, we are going to see a film and I am really looking forward to meeting her again. And, guess what, I am not going to mess it _____ again.

90

Solution

I   Synonyms, opposites and word families

> *Hinweis: Versuche beim Vokabellernen immer neue Wörter mit bereits be-*
> *kannten zu vernetzen, indem du beispielsweise Synonyme, Gegenteile oder*
> *auch andere Wörter derselben Wortfamilie suchst. Auch die Kenntnis von*
> *Wortbildungsregeln erleichtert dir die Integration neuer Vokabeln in deinen*
> *fremdsprachlichen Wortschatz. Bei Schwierigkeiten und Unklarheiten arbeite*
> *mit einem einsprachigen Wörterbuch. (Hier ist es besonders von Vorteil,*
> *wenn du weißt, welche Abkürzungen im Wörterbuch verwendet werden.)*

1. courage
   adjective: **courageous**
   verb: **to encourage**
   opposite of verb: **to discourage**

2. to grow
   noun: **growth**
   adjective: **growing; grown**
   synonym of verb: **to increase (in size, number, strength, height or quality)**

3. obedience
   verb: **to obey**
   adjective: **obedient**
   opposite of noun: **disobedience**

4. memorable
   noun: **memory, memorial, memorabilia, memoir(s)**
   verb: **to remember, to memorise, to memorialise**

5. offence
   verb: **to offend**
   adjective: **offensive**
   noun: **offender, offensiveness, offence**

6. to respond
   noun: **response**
   opposite of verb: **to ask, to inquire, to question**
   synonym: **to answer, to reply, to react (etc.)**

II   Phrasal and prepositional verbs

Hinweis: *Die Verwendung von Adverbien und Präpositionen bei den soge-*
nannten phrasal *und* prepositional verbs *bereitet Englischlernenden oft*
besondere Schwierigkeiten. Achte also beim Vokabellernen immer darauf,
dass du die korrekte Ergänzung mit lernst. Einige Verben können mit
mehreren Adverbien und Präpositionen gebraucht werden, haben dann aber
jeweils eine andere Bedeutung.

Three weeks ago, I asked **out** that girl from my class. Her name is Angela and she is really beautiful. And, believe it or not, she did not turn me **down**, but she actually showed **up** for our date. And she looked gorgeous. The T-shirt she was wearing really brought **out** the colour of her eyes …

Well, we went to an amusement park and had a great time together. We really hit it **off**. I even took some pictures. First I was afraid that there wasn't enough light, but they actually turned **out** great.

After that first date, we agreed to go out again. But I didn't dare to ring her **up**. Well, if you want to tell me **off** and say that I am an idiot, you are right. Last Wednesday, I ran **into** her in the grocer's shop and the situation was completely embarrassing. Nevertheless, we talked for a while and it turned **out** that she was really depressed because she had not done well in her last exams. So I decided not to miss **out** on the chance to cheer her **up** and I told her that I wanted to take her **out** to the cinema.

Today, we are going to see a film and I am really looking forward to meeting her again. And, guess what, I am not going to mess it **up** again.

Notenschlüssel:

1	2	3	4	5	6
24–21	20–18	17–15	14–12	11–8	7–0

20 minutes

The long walk home

The writer Doris Pilkington grew up believing that her mother had deliberately abandoned her at the age of four in a forbidding[1] state-run institution far away from her family, her people and her birthplace in the Western Australian desert.

"I really resented her. The thought that my mother just gave me away haunted
5 and tormented[2] me."

At the Moore River Native Settlement north of Perth – a cheerless internment camp for cross-breed[3] Aboriginal children – the windows were barred and any child who attempted escape was punished with solitary confinement[4]. Here, Doris's native tongue – Mardujara – was beaten out of her. [...]

10 Now 65 – an imposing[5] grey-haired figure, whose floral dress and silver jewellery suggest a certain bohemian[6] grandeur – Doris clearly remembers the day 40 years ago when she was finally reunited with her mother, Molly Craig, and first learned the truth.

Far from being abandoned, she had been stolen, forcibly separated from her
15 mother as part of an official government policy to "assimilate" half-castes and quarter-castes[7] into white Australia and train them to enter "civilised" society as servants and labourers.

"When I confronted my mother about it, when I asked her why she had deserted me, my mum just broke down.

20 "She said, 'I didn't give you away, the government took you away. And it hurt me so much to have to leave you.' It was such a moving moment between us. That is when I decided to learn more about my own culture, and to research the policies and the politics that had affected our lives."

Doris's decision took her on a long journey of self-discovery, during which she
25 learnt that she had no monopoly on childhood suffering: her mother had been through exactly the same misery at Moore River Native Settlement – with one key difference. Molly escaped.

In 1931, the 14-year-old Molly seized her little sister Daisy and her cousin Gracie by the hand and walked more than 1,000 miles home across baking desert
30 to the outback station of Jigalong, taking as her guide the immense rabbit-proof fence[8] that crossed the desert.

The girls' extraordinary trek – as written up by Doris in her acclaimed 1996 book, *Follow the Rabbit-Proof Fence* – has now been turned into a controver-

sial, moving and highly praised film which tackles one of the ugliest aspects of
35 recent Australian history. […]

The English-born Neville[9] was the prime mover behind the half-caste removals,
believing that the offspring of Aboriginal women and white men belonged with
their fathers' race.

The underlying purpose of the policy he enforced, which affected tens of thou-
40 sands of mixed-race Australians between 1905 and 1971, was to encourage miscegenation[10] between "near-white" females and white males, thus stealthily[11]
and systematically breeding out[12] the darkness of Australia's indigenous people.
The process, which has been described as attempted genocide, created what are
now known as the Stolen Generations. […]

45 Doris insists the film has done a "great job" of telling her family's story […].

The film, like Doris's book, climaxes with Molly's triumphant return home. But
reality was messier and more complex. On her return Molly married an Aboriginal man and had two children: Doris and Annabelle.

She was then taken back to Moore River with her children. Molly again escaped
50 – making the same extraordinary journey for a second time, this time with her
baby in her arms; but she was unable to rescue Doris and had to leave her behind. […]

As for herself, Doris says: "I've reclaimed my history, my culture, my family.
But my journey, my healing will only end when I am able to read and write in my
55 own language. Otherwise my mother's language could die with her." […]

from "The long walk home" by Demetrios Matheou.   *(605 words)*
http://www.telegraph.co.uk/culture/4728661/The-long-walk-home.html

Annotations
1 forbidding – unpleasant, threatening
2 tormented – tortured
3 cross-breed – here: children who have got an Aboriginal mother and a white father (or the other
   way around)
4 solitary confinement – the isolation of one child in a separate cell as a punishment
5 imposing – impressive
6 bohemian – unconventional
7 half-castes and quarter-castes – people of mixed race or ethnicity, i. e. someone with one white
   parent (half-caste) or someone with one Aboriginal grandfather or grandmother (quarter-caste)
8 rabbit-proof fence – a fence that was constructed in Australia between 1901 and 1907 in order to
   keep rabbits from the east out of the western part
9 Neville – the "Chief Protector of Aborigines" who was responsible for the girls' removal from
   their families
10 miscegenation – the mixture of races (e. g. through marriage)
11 stealthily – secretly
12 to breed out – to eliminate by means of controlled reproduction

I Multiple choice (9 pts)

Tick the correct answer. Several answers may be correct.

1. Doris Pilkington was …

   ☐ abandoned by her mother at the age of four and given to a state-run children's home.

   ☐ born in the Western Australian desert.

   ☐ not allowed to speak her native Aboriginal language at the Moore River Native Settlement.

2. The Moore River Native Settlement was …

   ☐ a private school for children with one Aboriginal and one white parent.

   ☐ constructed in order to train non-white Australian children to become part of white society as servants and labourers.

   ☐ an internment camp for mixed-race children who had been taken away from their parents according to a political decision.

3. The official government policy at that time …

   ☐ was the result of the prevailing opinion that the children of Aboriginal mothers and white fathers belonged with the white race.

   ☐ actually intended to eliminate the Aboriginal people in Australia.

   ☐ affected only few Aboriginal families.

II Summarising the text (11 pts)

Complete the summary of Molly Craig's life.

At the age of 14, Molly, Daisy and Gracie managed _____

from _____

and _____

following the rabbit-proof fence.

After having returned home, Molly _____

and _____.

When she was taken back to Moore River, Molly _____

_____.

She took _____.

95

But she couldn't _____.

More than 20 years later, Doris found her and Molly explained to her

that _____ but _____

_____ by _____.

Solution

The long walk home

I Multiple choice

1. Doris Pilkington was …

   ☐ abandoned by her mother at the age of four and given to a state-run children's home.

   ☑ born in the Western Australian desert.

   ☑ not allowed to speak her native Aboriginal language at the Moore River Native Settlement.

2. The Moore River Native Settlement was …

   ☐ a private school for children with one Aboriginal and one white parent.

   ☑ constructed in order to train non-white Australian children to become part of white society as servants and labourers.

   ☑ an internment camp for mixed-race children who had been taken away from their parents according to a political decision.

3. The official government policy at that time …

   ☑ was the result of the prevailing opinion that the children of Aboriginal mothers and white fathers belonged with the white race.

   ☑ actually intended to eliminate the Aboriginal people in Australia.

   ☐ affected only few Aboriginal families.

II Summarising the text

Hinweis: Hier hast du einige Wörter einer Textzusammenfassung vorliegen, die du um die entsprechenden Informationen aus dem Text ergänzen sollst. Achte darauf, dass der Text, den du einfügst, grammatikalisch fehlerfrei an die Vorgaben anschließt und gib so viele Details wie möglich wieder (z. B. Eigennamen).

At the age of 14, Molly, Daisy and Gracie managed **to escape from the Moore River Native Settlement** and **to walk back home across the desert** following the rabbit-proof fence.

After having returned home, Molly **married an Aboriginal man** and **had two daughters**.

When she was taken back to Moore River, Molly **managed to escape a second time.** She took **her baby daughter with her**. But she couldn't **save Doris**.

More than 20 years later, Doris found her and Molly explained to her that **she had not abandoned her** but **had been forced to leave her by the government**.

Notenschlüssel:

1	2	3	4	5	6
20–18	17–15	14–12	11–10	9–7	6–0

20 minutes

Der Girls'Day – Mädchen-Zukunftstag

An jedem vierten Donnerstag im April […] öffnen vor allem technische Unternehmen, Betriebe mit technischen Abteilungen und Ausbildungen, Hochschulen und Forschungszentren in ganz Deutschland ihre Türen für Schülerinnen ab der Klasse 5.

5 Die Mädchen lernen am Girls'Day Ausbildungsberufe und Studiengänge in Technik, IT, Handwerk und Naturwissenschaften kennen, in denen Frauen bisher eher selten vertreten sind oder begegnen weiblichen Vorbildern in Führungspositionen aus Wirtschaft oder Politik.

Der Girls'Day ist das größte Berufsorientierungsprojekt für Schülerinnen. Seit
10 dem Start der Aktion im Jahr 2001 haben bei einer stetig steigenden Zahl an Veranstaltungen insgesamt über 1 000 000 Mädchen teilgenommen. […]

Warum ein Zukunftstag für Mädchen?

Die junge Frauengeneration in Deutschland verfügt über eine besonders gute Schulbildung. Dennoch entscheiden sich Mädchen im Rahmen ihrer Ausbil-
15 dungs- und Studienwahl noch immer überproportional häufig für „typisch weibliche" Berufsfelder oder Studienfächer. Damit schöpfen sie ihre Berufsmöglichkeiten nicht voll aus; den Betrieben aber fehlt gerade in technischen und techniknahen Bereichen zunehmend qualifizierter Nachwuchs. […]

Was passiert am Girls'Day?

20 Technische Unternehmen und Abteilungen, sowie Hochschulen, Forschungszentren und ähnliche Einrichtungen bieten am Girls'Day Veranstaltungen für Mädchen an und tragen diese im Vorfeld auf der Aktionslandkarte unter www.girls-day.de ein. Unternehmen und Organisationen öffnen am Aktionstag alle Bereiche, in denen Frauen bislang unterrepräsentiert sind. Die Teilnehme-
25 rinnen erleben z. B. in Laboren, Büros und Werkstätten wie interessant und spannend diese Arbeit sein kann. In Workshops und bei Aktionen gewinnen die Mädchen Einblick in die Praxis verschiedenster Bereiche der Arbeitswelt und erproben praktisch ihre Fähigkeiten im technischen Bereich. Sie erhalten direkte Antworten auf ihre Fragen und können erste Kontakte knüpfen.
30 Auch geht es darum, die Öffentlichkeit und Wirtschaft auf die Stärken der Mädchen aufmerksam zu machen, um einer gut ausgebildeten Generation junger Frauen weit reichende Zukunftsperspektiven zu eröffnen. Unternehmen, die er-

folgreich spezielle „Mädchen-Tage" realisierten, verzeichnen einen steigenden Anteil junger Frauen in technischen und techniknahen Berufen.

35 Auswirkungen

Für viele junge Frauen hat die Zukunft in einem technischen Ausbildungs- oder Studiengang aufgrund ihrer Teilnahme am Girls'Day bereits begonnen. Evaluationsergebnisse bestätigen, dass der Girls'Day positiven Einfluss auf das Image von technischen Berufen bei den Teilnehmerinnen hat und Unternehmen ent-
40 wickeln durch die Teilnahme am Girls'Day ein verstärktes Engagement bei der Ansprache von jungen Frauen für technische Berufe.

Und die Jungen?

Für Jungen ab der 5. Klasse findet parallel zum Girls'Day der Boys'Day – Jungen-Zukunftstag statt. Bundesweit laden Einrichtungen, Organisationen,
45 Schulen und Hochschulen sowie Unternehmen Schüler ab der 5. Klasse ein. Sie lernen an diesem Tag Dienstleistungsberufe z. B. in den Bereichen Erziehung, Soziales, Gesundheit und Pflege kennen sowie weitere Berufsfelder, in denen bislang wenige Männer arbeiten. Oder sie besuchen Angebote zu den Themen Lebensplanung und soziale Kompetenzen. […]   *(426 words)*

Bundesweite Koordinierungsstelle Girls'Day – Mädchen-Zukunftstag © 2001–2010
Kompetenzzentrum Technik – Diversity – Chancengleichheit e.V.
http://www.girls-day.de/Girls_Day_Info

Mediation   (30 pts)

Du beherbergst Kevin, einen amerikanischen Gastschüler, der nach Deutschland gekommen ist, um Deutsch zu lernen. Bei einem Ausflug in die Stadt sieht er ein Plakat, auf dem groß „Girls'Day" steht und amüsiert sich darüber, dass es in Deutschland einen Tag extra für Mädchen gibt. Natürlich will er wissen, was das ist. Wieder zu Hause gehst du auf die „Girls'Day"-Website und beantwortest ihm seine Fragen – natürlich auf Englisch.

Vervollständige den Dialog.

KEVIN: So, what is "Girls'Day"?

YOU: _____

_____

_____

_____

_____

_____

_____

_____

_____

_____

_____

_____

KEVIN: Why is that necessary?

YOU: _____

_____

_____

_____

_____

_____

_____

_____

KEVIN: What do they do on "Girls'Day"?

YOU: _____

_____

_____

_____

_____

_____

_____

_____

_____

_____

_____

KEVIN: Well, all that sounds OK, but is it successful?

YOU: _____

_____

_____

_____

_____

_____

_____

_____

_____

_____

KEVIN: Sounds good for the girls. But what about the boys?

YOU: _____

_____

_____

_____

_____

_____

_____

_____

_____

KEVIN: So, equal rights for girls and boys at last.

Solution

Der Girls'Day – Mädchen-Zukunftstag

Mediation

Hinweis: Bei einer Mediation sollst du die wichtigsten Aspekte eines Textes in deinen eigenen Worten in der jeweils anderen Sprache zusammenfassen. Dabei ist es wichtig, dass du die Rahmenbedingungen beachtest, d. h. für wen überträgst du den Text und weshalb. Die vorgegebene Situation gibt dir wichtige Hinweise, was den Stil deiner Antwort angeht. Bei der vorliegenden Aufgabe handelt es sich um einen Dialog, d. h., du solltest deinen Text dem mündlichen Sprachgebrauch anpassen (z. B. Kurzformen, Füllwörter) und auf die Aussagen des Gesprächspartners eingehen..

KEVIN: So, what is "Girls'Day"?

YOU: Once a year, at the end of April, girls from year 5 up are invited to take a look around technical enterprises, businesses with technical departments and technical training facilities, universities and research centres. This way, girls get to learn about professions and activities that are usually not chosen as careers by women. They also get to know female role models in leadership positions in business and politics.

KEVIN: Why is that necessary?

YOU: Well, it says here that although nowadays girls are very well educated, they still tend to choose occupations or courses of studies that could be called "typically female". But since an increasing number of enterprises need technically skilled trainees, girls should be encouraged to consider these career options as well.

KEVIN: What do they do on "Girls'Day"?

YOU: The companies and institutions taking part organise presentations, activities and workshops for girls, especially in those fields in which women have been underrepresented so far. So the girls can try out their abilities in practice and establish their first contacts. On an interactive website they can look up which enterprises are participating in the campaign.

KEVIN: Well, all that sounds OK, but is it successful?

YOU: Oh, yes, it says here that more and more young women who took part in "Girls'Day" have started jobs in professions that are related to technology or have chosen to do technical studies. And companies seem to be more sensitive about recruiting young women for technical jobs.

KEVIN: Sounds good for the girls. But what about the boys?

YOU: Oh, look, I didn't know that. There is also a "Boys'Day". It's virtually the same for boys, only in a different field: boys from year 5 up are invited to learn more about service occupations in the social, educational or healthcare fields or about other occupations in which men have been underrepresented so far.

KEVIN: So, equal rights for girls and boys at last.

Notenschlüssel:

1	2	3	4	5	6
30–27	26–23	22–19	18–15	14–10	9–0

20 minutes

Lecture or interactive teaching? New study of an old issue (Track 4)

I   **Listening for the gist**   (2 pts)

You are going to listen to a report about a study on interactive teaching methods.

Finish the sentences by ticking the correct statements. Several answers may be correct.

1. The study was carried out in two classes …

☐ of an introductory physics course at university.

☐ of different ability.

☐ that had been taught by good professors before.

2. The study …

☐ was part of a larger research project.

☐ confirmed earlier findings about lecturing to large classes.

☐ provoked criticism.

II **Listening for details**   (13 pts)

1. Give the correct information.

While in one class, the professor held on to _____

_____, the professor from the other class was

replaced by two teachers who had little teaching experience, but

were trained _____.

2. Decide whether the statements are true or false. Correct them if they are false.

                                                            true   false

a) The students in the second group were given   ☐   ☐
     tasks to accomplish before the next class.

     _____

     _____

		true	false
b)	When the two classes were tested after the experiment, the students in the interactive class performed better than the others.	☐	☐
	_____		
	_____		
c)	The students in the interactive class often could not solve a given problem.	☐	☐
	_____		
	_____		
d)	Professor Wieman has influenced the results.	☐	☐
	_____		
	_____		
e)	The study proves that the teacher's personality is more important than the teaching methods chosen.	☐	☐
	_____		
	_____		

III Comment   (15 pts)

Lectures, group discussions, role plays, individual presentations – which of these methods do you prefer personally and why?

Give your opinion and the reasons in about 150 words.

Solution

Lecture or interactive teaching? New study of an old issue (Tapescript)

This is the VOA Special English Education Report.

Professors have lectured for centuries. But how effective is lecturing to students compared to working with them?

A new study compared two classes of a beginning physics course at the University of British Columbia in Canada. There were more than two hundred sixty students in each section. Both were taught by popular and experienced professors.

The study took place for one week near the end of the school year. One class continued to be taught in the traditional lecture style. The other professor was replaced by two teachers. They had little teaching experience but received training in interactive teaching methods. The training was led by Carl Wieman, a Nobel Prize-winning physicist who leads a science education program.

There was almost no lecturing. The teachers put the students in small groups to discuss and answer questions. They gave them readings and quizzes to finish before class so they would come prepared to discuss the material.

Professor Wieman says before the experiment with these and other activities, test scores for both classes were the same.

CARL WIEMAN: "There was a great deal of careful data collected showing how identical the two sections, these two large sections of this class were beforehand. And this focused very much on looking at exactly what could be learned with the different methods from the classroom experience, the time when you have the maximum instructor interaction, or face-to-face interaction time."

Afterward, both classes took the same test. Students in the interactive class scored nearly twice as high as those in the traditional class. Attendance also increased that week.

Graduate student Ellen Schelew was one of the teachers. She says the methods they used are designed to encourage students to think like scientists.

ELLEN SCHELEW: "Their brains are turned on. They're thinking hard and they're really working through these problems. So even if they don't have enough time to complete a given problem, they are prepared to learn from the instructor feedback that always follows groups' tasks."

The study appeared in May in the journal Science. It seems to confirm earlier findings about lecturing to large classes. But some experts have criticized the way the study was done.

Both of the researchers who taught the class, Ms. Schelew and Louis Deslauriers, were also authors of the study. This could raise questions about whether their involvement might have influenced the results.

Professor Wieman is currently on leave from the University of British Columbia and the University of Colorado. He is the associate director for science in the White House Office of Science and Technology Policy.

He says research has shown better ways to teach based on evidence about how the brain learns. And he hopes more professors will learn that how someone teaches may be more important than who does the teaching.

And that's the VOA Special English Education Report. I'm Christopher Cruise.

VOA Voice of America, http://www.voanews.com/learningenglish/home/Lecture-or-Interactive-Teaching-Old-Issue-New-Study-122988678.html

I   Listening for the gist

1. The study was carried out in two classes …

   ☒ of an introductory physics course at university.

   ☐ of different ability.

   ☒ that had been taught by good professors before.

2. The study …

   ☐ was part of a larger research project.

   ☒ confirmed earlier findings about lecturing to large classes.

   ☒ provoked criticism.

II   Listening for details

1. While in one class, the professor held on to **the traditional lecture style**, the professor from the other class was replaced by two teachers who had little teaching experience, but were trained **in interactive teaching methods**.

		true	false
2. a)	The students in the second group were given tasks to accomplish before the next class.	☒	☐
b)	When the two classes were tested after the experiment, the students in the interactive class performed better than the others.	☒	☐
c)	The students in the interactive class often could not solve a given problem.	☐	☒

Sometimes the students in the interactive class did not have enough time to solve a problem but they worked hard, learnt a lot by thinking about it, and were ready to learn from the instructor feedback.

	true	false

d) Professor Wieman has influenced the results.   ☐   **☒**
There could be a problem because the authors of the study were the teachers of the interactive class. This might have influenced the results but there is no evidence to show this.

e) The study proves that the teacher's personality is more   ☐   **☒**
important than the teaching methods chosen.
The study proves that teaching methods are more important than the teacher's personality.

III Comment

Hinweis: Hier geht es darum, dass du deine Meinung zum Thema ausdrückst und möglichst gut begründest. Im Folgenden findest du eine mögliche Ant-wort. Natürlich kannst du dich auch für jede andere Unterrichtsmethode ent-scheiden, wenn du dies entsprechend begründest.

My favourite teaching method is lecturing because this method ensures that the teacher provides all the required knowledge on the topic. It is a time-saving method since the teacher can explain the important points and answer all ques-tions immediately. But, of course, the teacher must not only stand in front of the class and read out his/her notes, but also involve the students in the learning process and check whether they have understood what he/she has just said by asking them questions.

Nevertheless, it is quite interesting to have group discussions for a change. It in-creases student participation and makes them exchange their ideas. However, I have to say that usually only the self-confident students participate; for the rest it takes quite an effort to speak out in front of the others. In addition, some teachers do group discussions all the time, which is simply too much for us because we have long days at school and cannot always be active and creative.

Notenschlüssel:

1	2	3	4	5	6
30–27	26–23	22–19	18–15	14–10	9–0

20 minutes

Football is my life!

I   Inversion   (24 pts)

Rewrite the following sentences using an inversion without changing the meaning.

1. I had hardly sat down in front of the television when the teams started to sing the national anthems.

   _____

   _____

2. The referee showed the player the yellow card. He realised only later that this was the wrong decision.
   The referee showed the player the yellow card. _____

   _____

   _____

3. The player did not only have to leave the field immediately, but he was also banned from the next game.

   _____

   _____

4. The football rules must on no account be ignored.

   _____

   _____

5. The German team did not score a single goal. The English one did not score a goal either.
   The German team did not score a single goal. _____

   _____

   _____

6. If one of the teams had scored a goal, the match would not have ended in a draw.

_____

_____

7. The world championship had never before been won by this team.

_____

_____

8. The players are in no way responsible for the behaviour of the hooligans.

_____

_____

9. Nobody has scored so many goals for his team since 1956.

_____

_____

10. I did not feel relieved until the referee blew the final whistle.

_____

_____

11. I was so happy that I cried.

_____

_____

12. My friend was little aware of the importance of this game.

_____

_____

II Subjunctive   (14 pts)

Complete the text with the correct form of the verb in parentheses (tense, active or passive). Use the subjunctive where possible.

The current coach _____ (to announce, already) that he _____ (not to be) available

for the next season: "I wish I _____ (to be) able
to continue, but health issues _____ (to force)
me to quit my job," he says regretfully. So now, the club
_____ (to look for) a new coach.

The club president insists that the new coach _____
(to be) a former player of the national team: "It's essential that he
_____ (to know) how to motivate our players.
Apart from that it is crucial that he _____ (to
respect) by our players."

Of course, it _____ (to take) more than just know-
ledge of the game of football to be a great coach. Effective communication is vital in order to encourage the players.

Asked what they think makes a good coach, the players recommend
that the coach _____ (to insist) on discipline and
rules but, at the same time, _____ (not to forget)
to have fun and make practice exciting and motivating.

It is essential that somebody _____ (to be) in this
important position before official training _____
(to start) again at the end of May.

The club asks that prospective coaches _____
(to call) Manager Brian Smith for an informal chat on 555 30 701.

Solution

Football is my life!

I   Inversion

1. Hardly had I sat down in front of the television when the teams started to sing the national anthems.

2. Only later did he realise that this was the wrong decision.

3. Not only did the player have to leave the field immediately, but he was also banned from the next game.

4. On no account must the football rules be ignored.

5. Neither/Nor did the English one.

6. Had one of the teams scored a goal, the match would not have ended in a draw.

7. Never before had the world championship been won by this team.

8. In no way are the players responsible for the behaviour of the hooligans.

9. Not since 1956 has anybody scored so many goals for his team.

10. Not until the referee blew the final whistle did I feel relieved.

11. So happy was I that I cried.

12. Little was my friend aware of the importance of this game.

II   Subjunctive

Hinweis: Hier soll wenn möglich der subjunctive *verwendet werden. Er wird in der Alltagssprache kaum noch gebraucht und kommt heute vor allem in gehobenem* American English *vor. Seine Form entspricht immer dem Infinitiv des Verbs, d. h. auch in der 3. Person Singular wird kein -s angehängt.*

Der present subjunctive *wird in Nebensätzen verwendet, die mit* that *eingeleitet werden und eine Aufforderung oder einen Wunsch ausdrücken. Außerdem steht er in formelhaften Wendungen wie* „God save the Queen".

Der past subjunctive *findet sich ebenfalls in Wunschsätzen und du kennst ihn von der Wendung* „If I were you".

The current coach **has already announced** that he **will not be** available for the next season: "I wish I **(was)/were** able to continue, but health issues **force** me to quit my job," he says regretfully. So now, the club **is looking for** a new coach.

113

The club president insists that the new coach **be** a former player of the national team: "It's essential that he **know** how to motivate our players. Apart from that it is crucial that he **be respected** by our players."

Of course, it **takes** more than just knowledge of the game of football to be a great coach. Effective communication is vital in order to encourage the players.

Asked what they think makes a good coach, the players recommend that the coach **insist** on discipline and rules but, at the same time, **not forget** to have fun and make practice exciting and motivating.

It is essential that somebody **be** in this important position before official training **starts** again at the end of May.

The club asks that prospective coaches **call** Manager Brian Smith for an informal chat on 555 30 701.

Notenschlüssel:

1	2	3	4	5	6
38–34	33–29	28–24	23–19	18–12	11–0

20 minutes

Trash on Mount Everest   (Track 5)

I   Listening for details   (5 pts)

1.   While listening to the audio track, complete the text.

There it stands, on the border of _____ and _____,

_____ meters high. Some natives call it Chomolungma, or

"_____". But most people know

it as Mount Everest, the _____.

2.   Name five of the things that have been left up on Mount Everest.   (5 pts)

- _____
- _____
- _____
- _____
- _____

3.   Explain why it is so difficult to climb Mount Everest. Refer to …   (6 pts)
  a)   the weather:

  _____

  _____

  _____

  _____

  b)   oxygen:

  _____

  _____

  _____

  _____

II Multiple choice   (6 pts)

Tick the correct statements.

☐ Apa Sherpa[1], Dawa Steven Sherpa, and their team were hired by the government to remove the rubbish from Mount Everest.

☐ They are paid by the weight of the objects they bring down.

☐ There have been other attempts to clean Mount Everest, but they were not successful.

☐ Apa Sherpa's team is the first to remove rubbish from above eight thousand metres. The Sherpa do not usually enter the "Death Zone" because of the thin air and the cold.

☐ Apa Sherpa holds the record for the most climbs of Mount Everest.

Annotations

1   The Sherpa people are a group who live in the Himalayan area. They are famous for their skill at climbing mountains.

Solution

Trash on Mount Everest (Tapescript)

Hinweis: Sicherlich hast du schon vom höchsten Berg der Welt, dem Mount Everest gehört. Wenn du also die Überschrift dieser Hörverstehensübung liest, kannst du bereits eine ganze Menge Vorwissen aktivieren, das dir dann beim Verständnis des englischen Textes helfen wird. Achte jedoch darauf, dass du dich bei der Beantwortung der Fragen strikt auf das beschränkst, was du wirklich dem Text entnehmen kannst.

FAITH LAPIDUS: There it stands, on the border of Nepal and Tibet, eight thousand eight hundred fifty meters high. Some natives call it Chomolungma, or "Goddess Mother of the World." But most people know it as Mount Everest, the highest mountain on earth.

The sky near the top is a beautiful blue color. New snow lies deep and white. Everything is clear and cold and clean. Or, at least, it once was clean. That was before people began to climb the mountain and leave behind thousands of kilograms of trash!

But help is on the way. Two mountain climbers from Nepal are leading a team that hopes to remove much of the trash.

BOB DOUGHTY: What kind of things have been left up there? The list is long. There are temporary shelters, ropes, oxygen bottles, clothing, sleeping bags, food … and bodies! Over two hundred people have died trying to climb Mount Everest. Many of their bodies are still there, completely frozen.

This all started in nineteen twenty-one. British climbers were the first to try to reach the place called "the top of the world." They quickly discovered that going up was hard work. But getting back down safely was even more difficult. The first problem is the weather. It can change quickly. The temperature can quickly drop to forty degrees below zero Celsius. Winds can reach hurricane speed. Fingers and toes freeze, even if they are covered in thick, protective material.

FAITH LAPIDUS: The next big worry is the lack of oxygen in the air. The higher a climber goes, the thinner the air. Areas near the top of the mountain have only about thirty percent of the oxygen found at sea level.

What climbers have learned is that they must carry a lot of oxygen bottles and other supplies up the mountain if they ever hope to reach the top. But because of the cold weather and lack of oxygen, many climbers become very sick. Getting off the mountain alive is hard enough. Cleaning up all the trash on the way down is nearly impossible.

BOB DOUGHTY: What about all those bodies left on Mount Everest? Why are they still there? Experts say it is because they are too heavy to bring down. Climbers are told that, if they get sick high on the mountain, or fall and break a bone, they

117

should not expect help. Many climbers have become so tired they have sat down to rest and never gotten up.

So Apa Sherpa, Dawa Steven Sherpa, and their team have decided to clean up the mountain. They will be paid a small amount for each kilogram of objects they bring down. But the team's leaders say the money is not important. They want to do this for their country, and the world.

FAITH LAPIDUS: There have been three other attempts in recent years to clean Mount Everest. But this is the first attempt at removing trash from the "Death Zone." That is the level above eight thousand meters. Up there, the thin air and cold can kill a person very quickly.

Apa Sherpa knows where to find much of the trash on Mount Everest. He has climbed to the top a record twenty times since nineteen ninety.

VOA Voice of America, http://www.voanews.com/learningenglish/home/science-technology/Mangrove-forests-Everest-NSF-121499174.html

I Listening for details

1. There it stands, on the border of **Nepal** and **Tibet**, **8 850** meters high. Some natives call it Chomolungma, or "**Goddess Mother of the World**". But most people know it as Mount Everest, the **highest mountain on earth**.

2. • temporary shelters / tents
   • ropes
   • oxygen bottles
   • clothing
   • sleeping bags
   • food
   • bodies

3. a) the weather: Sometimes the weather changes quickly and the temperature can drop suddenly. There can be strong winds. Fingers and toes can freeze in spite of shoes and gloves.

   b) oxygen: The higher up the mountain, the thinner the air becomes, so climbers have to take enough oxygen bottles with them in order to compensate for the lack of oxygen.

II Multiple choice

☐ Apa Sherpa, Dawa Steven Sherpa, and their team were hired by the government to remove the rubbish from Mount Everest.

☒ They are paid by the weight of the objects they bring down.

☐ There have been other attempts to clean Mount Everest, but they were not successful.

118

$\boxed{X}$ Apa Sherpa's team is the first to remove rubbish from above eight thousand metres. The Sherpa do not usually enter the "Death Zone" because of the thin air and the cold.

$\boxed{X}$ Apa Sherpa holds the record for the most climbs of Mount Everest.

Notenschlüssel:

1	2	3	4	5	6
22−20	19−17	16−14	13−11	10−7	6−0

45 minutes

Immigration

Push and Pull

Like many who came before
From distant corners of the globe
Pushed from home
5 Fleeing calamity[1]
Hunger, Poverty, War

The United States
Land of Dreams
Pulling those seeking a better life
10 Offering hope and optimism
To the downtrodden, the desperate

They've come to this New World
For several hundred years now
In crashing waves from different places at different times
15 Only to face new struggles
In a new land

"They're taking our jobs."
"They're stealing our money."
"They don't want to speak English."
20 "Send them all back to where they came from."
They've all taken turns bearing the brunt[2]

Eventually each group melds into the giant pot
Becoming a part of a new America
Time and time again
25 And the wave we have crashing over our shores now
Will, too

by John Myers, created on February 02, 2008;
http://www.helium.com/items/837371-poetry-immigration

Annotations
1 calamity – disaster and distress
2 to bear the brunt – to put up with the worst of something bad

121

I   Working with a poem   (40 pts)

1. What does "Push and Pull" (l. 1) refer to?
   Explain with the help of the title and the text.

2. What kind of "new struggles" (l. 15) do immigrants have to face
   in America according to the text?

3. Choose two figures of speech that the author uses in his poem
   and explain them briefly.

II   Cartoon analysis   (20 pts)

Describe this cartoon and analyse its message.
Write about 150 words.

Ed Fischer / cartoonstock.com

Solution

Immigration

I   Working with a poem

1. The title "Immigration" indicates that "Push and Pull" (l. 1) refers to the so-called push and pull factors, a geographical term used to describe the reasons why people leave the area they live in (push) and why they are attracted to another area (pull). The author of the poem mentions disaster, lack of food, poverty and war (cf. ll. 5/6) as push factors. The United States of America, on the other hand, offers several pull factors, above all the hope for a new and better life (cf. l. 9).

2. After arriving in the US, immigrants meet with various prejudices held by "native" Americans, culminating in the demand to send the newcomers back to their home countries (cf. l. 20). They are accused of taking jobs away (cf. l. 17) and stealing money (cf. l. 18). They are also blamed for not making the effort to learn English (cf. l. 19).

3. For hundreds of years, the United States has been the "Land of Dreams" (l. 8) for millions of immigrants. The author of the poem describes their influx as a wave, which is quite a common **metaphor** illustrating the fact that there have been groups of immigrants from "different places at different times" (l. 14), leaving their countries for the reasons mentioned above. The author uses the expression "in crashing waves" (l. 14) in order to hint at the destructive force that mass immigration can have. In this poem, the author also alludes to the **metaphor** of the "melting pot" in order to underline that, after some time, each of these groups of immigrants has adapted to those already living there, each time making a contribution to forming a new society (cf. l. 22).

    That the new life in the United States is not always easy for the newcomers is emphasised by the use of an **anaphora** describing all the flaws "they", i. e. the immigrants, have (cf. ll. 17 ff.): They take away jobs, they are thieves, they do not want to learn English. These three lines are arranged according to increasing importance (a stylistic device called *climax*) leading up to the point where the "native" Americans want to send them back again (cf. l. 20).

    At the end of the poem, the author picks up on the **metaphor** of the "wave" again when stating rather matter-of-factly that the latest wave of immigrants will also adapt to American society – as all the others did before. He stresses this conviction by writing only two words in the last line, thus ending on a reassuring note for the reader.

II Cartoon analysis

Hinweis: Bei der Analyse einer Karikatur kommt es darauf an, dass du zunächst genau beschreibst, was du siehst. Du kannst davon ausgehen, dass jedem Detail eine Bedeutung im Hinblick auf die Aussage der Karikatur zukommt, vernachlässige also nichts. Doch die Beschreibung alleine reicht nicht aus, du musst auch die Aussage der Karikatur möglichst umfassend darstellen.

In this cartoon, an illegal immigrant standing on top of a ladder is picking apples off a tree. In his left hand, he is holding a bag labelled "Profit $". He is looking anxiously towards a giant hand coming from behind him that apparently wants to sweep him off the ladder. The hand belongs to the US immigration authorities and seems to be moving towards him.

The cartoon illustrates the fact that immigrants who live illegally in the USA tend to work in low-wage jobs, such as picking crops or fruit. Since they are desperate to earn a living or feed their families, they work for lower wages and minimal benefits, thus enabling employers to make more money because cheaper labour costs and poor working conditions mean greater profits for the employers. So, the man in the cartoon works directly for the profit of his employer, who, however, will not protect him against the US immigration authorities symbolised by the giant hand. If the government detects illegal immigrants at work, they are deported back to their countries.

Notenschlüssel:

1	2	3	4	5	6
60–53	52–46	45–38	37–30	29–20	19–0

Klassenarbeit 2
Schwerpunkte: *Reading comprehension, grammar, writing*

45 minutes

Paying the price for our plastic world

It's the synthetic wonder that we can't live without – but how do we live with it?

TRY and go a day – scratch that, an hour – without touching plastic. Go on, bet you can't do it.

You won't be able to lean on your laminated benchtop, brush your teeth, pick up your shampoo bottle, button your shirt, […] touch your computer keyboard or
5 use the TV remote. Forget grabbing the keys and jumping in the car. And you'd probably have to go a little hungry too. Can't touch the fridge handle to get to the plastic wrapped bacon, tub of yoghurt or plastic bottle of juice. […]

Susan Freinkel set herself this very task and found she lasted until she had to use the toilet, just seconds into her experimental day. So the American author instead
10 decided to write down everything she touched made with plastic in all its forms (starting with her pen). By the end of the day she had filled four pages with a no-where-near exhaustive[1] list of 196 items […].

"I didn't really contemplate[2] what that would mean or how hard it might be until that morning … it opened my eyes to just how ubiquitous it was," says Freinkel,
15 a science journalist who has written a book *Plastic: A Toxic Love Story*. […]

Freinkel is not on any crusade[3]. In her view, plastic is neither all good nor all bad: it is simply a material.

"How we use it determines whether it's a good use or a bad use; how you make it determines whether it's a problem or not … when you put it into things that are
20 meant to last a long time, I have less trouble with that," she says. "I'm not advo-cating[4] giving up plastics. I'm just advocating using it in a more thoughtful fash-ion." […]

One of the worst is that we treat too much of this durable material as disposable – use once, throw away, repeat many times daily – when we should treat it like a
25 limited resource and recycle as much as possible.

Freinkel thinks cars, computers, even fridges, should not be stripped only for their valuable parts. The abundant[5] plastic they carry should also be returned to the production cycle. […]

She makes some sobering[6] observations: The world has produced almost as
30 much plastic in the past decade as we did for the whole of last century. […] In the space of a generation, the average American has gone from consuming about 13 kg of plastic items a year to 10 times that – about 136 kg. […]

More disturbing[7], but not all that surprising, is that "humans are just a little plastic now".

35 "Just as plastics changed the essential texture of modern life, so they are altering the basic chemistry of our bodies," writes Freinkel in her book.

Plastics has been with us since the 1830s, when a German apothecary discovered polystyrene – though it would be another 80 years before the world started to understand what it had in its hands. However, English inventor Alexander Parkes
40 is credited with the first man-made plastic – Parkesine – a cellulose-based material he created in the 1850s that held its shape until it was heated.

It was assumed, as our post-war love affair with plastics began to flourish, that it was inert[8], safe. Then, in the late '60s, scientists discovered that a key chemical used to make PVC pliable[9] – a phthalate – was leaching into humans from medi-
45 cal devices (such as blood transfusion bags) and everyday plastic products. It turns out phthalates – which are now being phased out of products in the US and Europe – easily leach into food and the atmosphere, especially in warmer conditions.

[…] The chemical has been linked to asthma, allergies and […] can in high doses
50 interfere with hormones and foetal development. […]

It is impossible to live a normal life that avoids all plastic. Even if you scrupulously avoid packaged food and anything that comes in plastic containers, there are non-negotiable items needed for everyday work and life, such as telephones […] and computers. […]

55 "I think we're reaching a tipping point … and either we deal with these problems or we face some pretty serious consequences," [Freinkel] says of the explosion in plastic production and waste.

"I don't think we have to accept a world in which we are inevitably threatened by the everyday products we use. I really think we ought to have a manufactur-
60 ing process and policies that support a process in which what goes into the marketplace is screened and found safe for health and the environment."

Having written her book, she is both more appreciative[10] and more concerned about plastics than she used to be. It has made her more careful about the choices and purchases she makes and she is more diligent[11] about recycling.

65 "It does get to you." *(779 words)*

Maria Moscaritolo: Paying the price for our plastic world. © News Limited, The Advertiser (June 11, 2011)

Annotations
1. exhaustive – comprehensive; considering all aspects
2. to contemplate – to think about sth.
3. crusade – a campaign against sth.
4. to advocate – to support; to speak in favour of
5. abundant – available in large quantities
6. sobering – tending to make one thoughtful
7. disturbing – worrying
8. inert – unable to act; passive
9. pliable – easily bent or shaped
10. appreciative – respectful
11. diligent – careful

I Working with the text   (50 pts)

1. Describe Susan Freinkel's experiment.
   Why and how did she have to change it?

2. Summarise Freinkel's opinion about plastic.

3. Point out the problems that the use of plastic has brought about for humans.

4. Explain whether the experiment changed Freinkel's attitude.
   What solution does she suggest?

II Adjectives and adverbs   (10 pts)

Complete the sentences with the correct form of the word in brackets: adjective or adverb.

1. There is an _____ (increasing) awareness of the benefits of waste recycling all over Europe.

2. Nowadays, with the amount of waste _____ (rapid) growing, people take green issues _____ (serious) and refuse to _____ (simple) throw things away.

3. Recycling of _____ (specific) materials has grown _____ (drastic) over the last few years.

4. The _____ (overall) success of recycling processes depends _____ (heavy) on people's willingness to separate their rubbish at home.

5. Mixed waste can be separated _____ (mechanic) or _____ (manual) at centralised sorting plants.

6. _____ (recent) studies show that thirty years ago householders _____ (rare) took their waste to bottle, can and paper banks.

7. Separate collection of waste has an _____ (important) effect on the householders' awareness of the impact of the waste that they create.

8. Recycling is a _____ (real) _____ (easy) way for every single person to make an _____ (individual) contribution.

9. The government also aims to limit the _____ (enormous) mountain of waste by _____ (insistent) encouraging industry to promote products that leave a minimum of waste after use.

10. There is still a _____ (great) deal of waste which could be recycled that ends up in landfill sites, which is _____ (harmful) to the environment.

III Composition   (30 pts)
Choose one of the following topics and write about 150 words.

1. Throw-away society.

2. As a member of the student council of your school, you want to draw your schoolmates' attention to the fact that if everybody participated in avoiding plastic in their everyday lives, this could make a change.
   Write a convincing speech, explaining two possibilities of avoiding plastic.

Solution

Paying the price for our plastic world

I Working with the text

1. Susan Freinkel's aim was not to touch plastic for one day. But since she could not even use the toilet without touching plastic, she changed the original task and instead noted down all the things made of plastic that she had to touch during the day.

2. Susan Freinkel neither supports nor condemns the use of plastic. For her, it is essential that the material is used in a responsible manner, i.e. it should be used in long-lasting things, and as much of it as possible should be recycled.

3. The fact that the consumption of plastic has increased ten times over the last ten years shows that plastic is really everywhere. It has even been found in human bodies. Scientists discovered that through medical devices and the use of everyday plastic products, phthalates enter the human body, causing respiratory diseases and allergies or having an impact on hormones and the development of foetuses.

4. The experiment made Susan Freinkel aware of the problems the use of plastic involves. Now she is more cautious about what she buys and she makes a point of recycling.
   She suggests that every product should be examined and found that it is completely safe to use and does not represent a health hazard. This should have an impact on the manufacturing process and on political and economic decisions.

II Adjectives and adverbs

1. There is an **increasing** awareness of the benefits of waste recycling all over Europe.

2. Nowadays, with the amount of waste **rapidly** growing, people take green issues **seriously** and refuse to **simply** throw things away.

3. Recycling of **specific** materials has grown **drastically** over the last few years.

4. The **overall** success of recycling processes depends **heavily** on people's willingness to separate their rubbish at home.

5. Mixed waste can be separated **mechanically** or **manually** at centralised sorting plants.

6. **Recent** studies show that thirty years ago householders **rarely** took their waste to bottle, can and paper banks.

7. Separate collection of waste has an **important** effect on the householders' awareness of the impact of the waste that they create.

8. Recycling is a **really easy** way for every single person to make an **individual** contribution.

9. The government also aims to limit the **enormous** mountain of waste by **insistently** encouraging industry to promote products that leave a minimum of waste after use.

10. There is still a **great** deal of waste which could be recycled that ends up in landfill sites, which is **harmful** to the environment.

III Composition

1. Throw-away society, consumer society – there seem to be a lot of names referring to the societies in industrialised countries. And the terms have a highly negative connotation.

   "To throw something away" means to get rid of something that is no longer needed or wanted. Every day, things are thrown away: packaging materials, old newspapers, food products – to name just a few.

   Curiously enough, it seems to be easier and cheaper nowadays to throw away things like broken TV sets rather than repair them. New clothes are bought and the old ones are thrown away – although they are still in good condition – just because they are no longer fashionable. People in developed countries have become accustomed to the fact that they are in a position to throw things away without much thought.

   But in our times, this throw-away mentality conflicts with the fact that in view of global warming and climate change people should waste less and use resources sparingly in order to save the environment. Instead, there is an excessive production of short-lived or disposable items, although the amount of waste produced by humans is increasing by the minute.

2. Ladies and gentlemen,

A few weeks ago, I saw a documentary about what is known as the Great Pacific Garbage Patch, a huge area of plastic trash floating in the Pacific Ocean. In the documentary, they stated that apart from the fact that this waste is a threat to marine wildlife, it enters the food chain so that every one of us already has a bit of plastic in their body.

We have to change something – now! If every one of us changes only a few of our habits, we can help to save our planet.

Let's start by avoiding plastic bags when we go shopping. Carry reusable shopping bags with you. This reduces the amount of packaging and is even cheaper for you since most supermarkets nowadays charge for plastic bags.

What is also good for your purse is taking your own reusable bottle or mug instead of using the disposable ones in the cafeteria or from the vending machine. Did you know that plastic may leach chemicals into the water? So why take a chance?

These small changes can help to make a big change – let's get started today! And here is something for you to think about: "Do you believe it's possible to live without plastic?"

Notenschlüssel:

1	2	3	4	5	6
90–79	78–68	67–57	56–45	44–30	29–0

45 minutes

I **Listening: A little light** (Track 6)

The text you are going to listen to is taken from a film by CEWEP, (20 pts)
the Confederation of European Waste-to-Energy Plants. Read all the
tasks first. Then listen to the text and complete the tasks.

1. Decide whether the statements are true or false. Correct them if
   they are false.

	true	false

   a) A reading light uses about 15 watts. ☐ ☐

   _____

   _____

   b) Waste that is produced all over Europe is trans- ☐ ☐
   formed into energy.

   _____

   _____

   c) It takes eight power plants to produce the energy ☐ ☐
   people need to use their reading lights.

   _____

   _____

   d) Waste-to-energy plants can only use waste that is ☐ ☐
   suitable for recycling.

   _____

   _____

2. While listening to the text, complete the following sentences.

   Half of our energy comes from _____, so it is

   _____ and doesn't affect _____.

Our energy already _____ 16 million tonnes of CO_2 every year. This is equal to the CO_2 produced by 7 million _____.

Our story of waste-to-energy has many highlights. Our energy runs through all of Europe, providing people with _____ and _____.

3. How is energy used in the different parts of Europe?
   Match the corresponding words and explanations.

City	Energy use	Company
I Amsterdam	**A** heating from heating network	**a** AEB Waste-to-Energy plant
II Nottingham	**B** warm water from heating network	**b** local Waste-to-Energy plant
III Munich	**C** power for tram, metro and city	**c** Eastcroft Waste-to-Energy plant

I		
II		
III		

II Working with a text

India's Poor Risk 'Slow Death' Recycling E-Waste

Young rag-pickers[1] sifting through rubbish are a common image of India's chronic poverty, but destitute children face new hazards picking apart old computers as part of the growing "e-waste" industry.

Asif, aged seven, spends his days dismantling electronic equipment in a
5 tiny, dimly-lit unit in east Delhi along with six other boys.
"My work is to pick out these small black boxes," he said, fingers deftly[2] prying out[3] integrated circuits from the pile of computer remains stacked high beside him.

His older brother Salim, 12, is also hard at work instead of being at school.
10 He is extracting tiny transistors and capacitors from wire boards.

The brothers, who decline to reveal how much they earn a day, say they are kept frantically[4] busy as increasing numbers of computers, printers and other electronic goods are discarded by offices and homes.

Few statistics are known about the informal "e-waste" industry, but a Unit-
15 ed Nations report launched in February described how mountains of hazard-
ous waste from electronic products are growing exponentially in developing
countries.

It said India would have 500 percent more e-waste from old computers in
2020 than in 2007, and 18 times more old mobile phones.

20 The risks posed to those who handle the cast-offs[5] are clear to T.K. Joshi,
head of the Centre for Occupational and Environmental Health at the
Maulana Azad Medical College in New Delhi.

He studied 250 people working in the city as recyclers and dismantlers over
12 months to October 2009 and found almost all suffered from breathing
25 problems such as asthma and bronchitis.

"We found dangerously high levels – 10 to 20 times higher than normal – of
lead, mercury and chromium in blood and urine samples," he told AFP.

"All these have a detrimental[6] effect on the respiratory[7], urinary and digestive[8] systems, besides crippling immunity and causing cancer."

30 Toxic metals and poisons enter workers' bloodstreams during the laborious
manual extraction process and when equipment is crudely[9] treated to collect
tiny quantities of precious metals.

"The recovery of metals like gold, platinum, copper and lead uses caustic
soda[10] and concentrated acids," said Joshi.

35 "Workers dip their hands in poisonous chemicals for long hours. They are
also exposed to fumes of highly concentrated acid."

Safety gear such as gloves, face masks and ventilation fans are virtually un-
heard of, and workers – many of them children – often have little idea of
what they are handling.

40 "All the workers we surveyed were unaware of the dangers they were exposed to. They were all illiterate[11] and desperate for employment," said
Joshi. "Their choice is clear – either die of hunger or of metal poisoning."

And he warned exposure to e-waste by-products such as cadmium and lead
could result in a slow, painful death.

45 "They can't sleep or walk," he said. "They are wasted by the time they
reach 35–40 years of age and incapable of working."

There are no estimates of how many people die in India from e-waste poisoning as ill workers generally drift back to their villages when they can no
longer earn a living.

50 "The irony is that the amounts of gold and platinum they extract are traces –
fractions of a milligram," said Priti Mahesh, program coordinator of the
New Delhi-based Toxic Link environment group. [...]

For Joshi, the sight of children working in appalling conditions taking computers apart is as potent a symbol of India's deep troubles as rag-pickers
55 sorting through stinking household rubbish dumps.

"India needs laws which will protect workers' interests, especially the vulnerable and children. We have a lot to learn from Western societies about workers' rights," he said. *(594 words)*

© AFP (11.07.2010)

Annotations
1   rag-picker – a person who makes a living by picking up and selling old clothes and other rubbish
2   deftly – done skilfully and quickly
3   to pry out – to remove sth. from sth.
4   frantically – wildly and excitedly
5   cast-off – sth. that has been thrown away
6   detrimental – causing damage
7   respiratory – relating to the process of breathing
8   digestive – relating to the process of digesting food
9   crudely – not carefully
10 caustic soda – *Natronlauge*
11 illiterate – unable to read or write

1.   Synonyms   (5 pts)
     Read the following text and find words in the text that have the same meaning as the following words.

     a)   very poor

     _____

     b)   danger

     _____

     c)   to refuse

     _____

     d)   to throw away

     _____

     e)   terrible

     _____

2. Paraphrases (5 pts)
Rewrite the following sentences from the text without using the underlined words.

a) "He is extracting tiny transistors and capacitors" (ll. 9/10)

_____

b) "a United Nations report launched in February" (ll. 14/15)

_____

c) "All the workers we surveyed were unaware of the dangers they were exposed to." (ll. 40/41)

_____

d) "the amounts of gold and platinum they extract are traces" (l. 50)

_____

e) "as potent a symbol of India's deep troubles" (l. 54)

_____

3. Questions on the text (40 pts)
Read all the questions first. Then answer them in the given order. Use your own words as far as appropriate.

a) Describe the "e-waste" industry in India.

b) Outline the consequences that working in the "e-waste" industry can have.

c) Explain the reasons why people work in the "e-waste" industry although they have to put up with these consequences.

4. Beyond the text (20 pts)
Give your personal opinion on the following questions and a short explanation for it. Write about four sentences.

a) Why is the dangerous waste treated in developing countries?

b) Why did India probably have to deal with 500 percent more e-waste in 2020?

Solution

A little light (Tapescript)

Hinweis: Bei diesem Hörverstehenstext handelt es sich um ein Werbevideo für die Energiegewinnung durch Müllverbrennung, d. h. diese Art der Energiegewinnung wird sehr positiv dargestellt. Dieses Vorwissen kann dir helfen, die entsprechenden Informationen aus dem Text zu entnehmen.

Reading a book, just before going to sleep is nice. When you're young, it takes all your energy. And about 15 watts for the reading light.

Some of this electricity is recovered from the waste that we all produce. This waste is transformed into precious energy by Waste-to-Energy plants.

In fact in Europe, we produce enough electricity to power eight reading lights in every household, every day of the year.

If we could use the waste that is not suitable for recycling, but is still buried today, then we could light as much as 14 reading lights in every household every day.

Half of our energy comes from biomass, so it is renewable and doesn't affect global warming.

Our energy already avoids 16 million tonnes of CO_2 every year. This is equal to the CO_2 produced by 7 million passenger cars.

Our story of waste-to-energy has many highlights. Our energy runs through all of Europe, providing people with heat and light.

A day out in Amsterdam (the Netherlands): electricity generated by the AEB Waste-to-Energy plant helps provide green certified power for the tram, metro and city.

Going ice skating is fun: in Nottingham (England) the National Ice Centre is on the city's district heating network, receiving energy generated by treating waste in the Eastcroft Waste-to-Energy plant.

The Glockenbrot bakery near Munich (Germany) emits 46 % less CO_2 than traditional bakeries by using innovative energy-efficient technologies such as warm water from the district heating network supplied by the local Waste-to-Energy plant.

In the winter 50 % of Paris (France), including the famous Louvre museum, is heated by three Waste-to-Energy plants, helping to keep the Mona Lisa smiling.

Waste-to-Energy has a lot to offer. If we can recover energy from waste, let's not waste this energy.

with the kind support of CEWEP

I Listening

			true	false
1.	a)	A reading light uses about 15 watts.	☒	☐
	b)	Waste that is produced all over Europe is transformed into energy.	☒	☐
	c)	It takes eight power plants to produce the energy people need to use their reading lights.	☐	☒

In Europe, waste-to-energy plants produce enough electricity to power eight reading lights in every household, every single day.

			true	false
	d)	Waste-to-energy plants can only use waste that is suitable for recycling.	☐	☒

Waste-to-energy plants use the waste that is not suitable for recycling.

2. Half of our energy comes from **biomass**, so it is **renewable** and doesn't affect **global warming**.
Our energy already **avoids** 16 million tonnes of CO_2 every year. This is equal to the CO_2 produced by 7 million **passenger cars**.
Our story of waste-to-energy has many highlights. Our energy runs through all of Europe, providing people with **heat** and **light**.

3.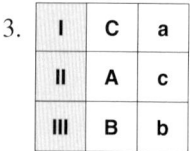

I	C	a
II	A	c
III	B	b

II Working with a text

1. Synonyms
   a) destitute (l. 2)
   b) hazard (l. 2)
   c) to decline (l. 11)
   d) to discard (l. 13)
   e) appalling (l. 53)

2. Paraphrases
   a) taking out / removing
   b) published
   c) not conscious
   d) quantities
   e) strong / powerful

3. Questions on the text
   a) Poor people, especially children, in India can earn a little bit of money by taking apart old computers and other technical devices and then extracting the valuable metals. Since more and more electronic products are thrown away, there are tonnes of "e-waste" that have to be dealt with.

   b) Working in the "e-waste" industry can cause severe damage to the workers' health. It can cause breathing problems and affect the urinary and digestive systems and the immune system. It can even cause cancer, for example, because of the poisonous substances that enter the workers' bloodstream or by the substances that are used to recover metals. It is not known how many people actually die from e-waste poisoning.

   c) Most of the workers are very poor, so they need the jobs in the "e-waste" industry to earn a living. They prefer this kind of work to starving. Since they are not able to read or write and many of them are still very young, they are not aware of the risks to their health. They do not know which substances they are exposed to.

4. Beyond the text
   a) Most of the electronic products are thrown away in industrialised countries, but there people know how dangerous it can be to take apart the different parts and extract the metal once the devices are no longer needed. So for the industrialised countries it is more convenient to get rid of the unwanted waste and ship it to India and other developing countries where workers are cheap and unaware of the risks – out of sight, out of mind. Additionally if the workers get sick in India, they have no lobby to fight for their rights, so the companies are not at risk of having to pay compensation for possible damage done to the health of their employees.

b) As computers, televisions and mobile phones have an increasingly short life-span, more of them are thrown away without hesitation by a society that can afford to buy the latest gadget at any time. In addition, more and more people have technical devices at their disposal. Hardly anybody thinks about their "afterlife", so the waste is taken to India, where it is taken care of.

Notenschlüssel:

1	2	3	4	5	6
90–79	78–67	66–56	55–45	44–30	29–0

45 minutes

Arranged marriages – first comes marriage, then comes love …

Sita is a dentist. She grew up in Delhi and, after qualifying, asked her parents to arrange her marriage. Sita explains why: "University made me think very differently about relationships. Opportunities came up but I didn't want them. I felt they were lacking in depth, in maturity[1]. If I had found someone, my parents
5 would have been happy but I wanted my family to be involved in the choice." So Sita was introduced to Praveen and within the first five hours, both of them knew that this was it. Without any complications and after only a few meetings, they were married. Sita feels that it is important for people to understand the difference between forced marriages, in which the partners are emotionally and
10 even physically coerced[2], and what she and Praveen had, an arrangement that gave them final choice.

By insisting on her parents choosing her partner, Sita kept to the Indian custom of arranged marriages. Many people raised in the western world might consider it strange that the Indians still hold on to this tradition, while India is on its way
15 to becoming in some respects a progressive and modernized country. "Love marriages" do happen in India but not very frequently yet. Given that marriage is one of the most crucial decisions and in view of the fact that divorce is frowned upon by most Indians, the careful choice of a suitable partner is vitally important. Thus, to help the young person, who should not be left alone with
20 such a significant decision, the family try to find a marriage partner who possesses certain traits. The importance of good family background and compatibility as far as upbringing and family is concerned are vital. Thus the parents will look for similar levels of education, matching cultures and religions, and, of course, financial stability. In a country as diverse as India, where different religions,
25 languages and castes play an essential role in everyday life, young people trust their parents to arrange a practical union between two people with comparable backgrounds. Thus, marriages in India usually do not take place outside one's community and marriages across different religions or castes are rare. So after exchanging pictures of the possible partners, the parents meet the boy/girl and
30 their family. While, in the past, the future bride and groom would not see each other until their wedding day, today, there is usually a short period of courtship during which the two can get together and talk in the presence of a third person. And, if either one of the two is opposed to getting married to the other one, the marriage is most certainly cancelled. *(442 words)*

Annotations
1 maturity – state of being fully developed
2 coerced – forced to do sth.

I Paraphrases (6 pts)

Paraphrase the underlined parts of the following sentences from the text.

1. "Opportunities came up but I didn't want them." (l. 3)

_____

_____

2. "they were lacking in depth" (l. 4)

_____

_____

3. "people raised in the western world" (l. 13)

_____

_____

II Synonyms (4 pts)

Provide a synonym for the following underlined words from the text.

1. "divorce is frowned upon by most Indians" (ll. 17/18)

_____

2. "a marriage partner who possesses certain traits" (ll. 20/21)

_____

III Questions on the text (40 pts)

Answer the following questions in complete sentences.
Use your own words as far as appropriate.

1. What were Sita's reasons for her decision to have an arranged marriage?

2. What is the difference between an arranged and a forced marriage?

3. Why do people in India still hold on to the custom of arranged marriages?

4. What do Indian parents look for when they want to pick a partner for their son or daughter?

IV Comment   (10 pts)

Comment on the title from a European point of view.
Write about six sentences.

V Composition   (20 pts)

Choose **one** of the following tasks and write about 150 words.

a) Would you want your parents to be involved in your choice of a
    partner? Why (not)?

b) Imagine you have fallen in love with someone and want to marry
    him/her, but the family of the person you love is completely
    against the marriage. You talk about the situation with your best
    friend. Write a dialogue.

Solution

Arranged marriages – first comes marriage, then comes love …

I Paraphrases

1. **I met some people I could have started a relationship with** but I didn't want them.

2. they **did not have enough** depth

3. people **brought up/who grew up/who have grown up** in the western world

II Synonyms

1. divorce is **disapproved of/not approved of** by most Indians

2. a marriage partner who possesses certain **qualities/characteristics/features**

III Questions on the text

1. During her time at university, Sita could have had several relationships but always doubted that they would last. She wanted her parents to participate in the process of finding a suitable partner for life.

2. Whereas in a forced marriage, the parents decide whom their son/daughter is to marry and the children do not have a choice, in an arranged marriage the marriage can be called off if one of the partners is not happy with the arrangement.

3. Indians think that finding a suitable partner is one of the most important decisions in life, not least because getting divorced is not socially acceptable in India. Thus, young people should be supported when choosing their marriage partner. It is the family's duty to look for somebody who is suitable for their son or daughter.

4. For Indian parents it is crucial to find somebody from a good family who shares the same religion, culture and language as their son or daughter. Comparable levels of education and financial status also play an important role. Most of these factors are influenced by the caste system. Although according to the government caste does not define people's lives as it used to, your education, job and, as a result, the person you marry very often still depends on the caste you are born into.

IV Comment

"First comes marriage, then comes love ..."

In an arranged marriage, there is only a very short period of courtship and the partners only meet in the presence of a third person. Only after marriage do the two of them have the chance to really get to know each other and – if they are lucky – to fall in love with each other. For someone brought up in Europe this seems particularly strange because here most people marry for love and they want to enjoy this very special time at the beginning of a relationship when they fall in love. Thus, for a European, it is exactly the opposite of the Indian way: first comes love, then comes marriage. Most people take their time to get to know their partner and his/her personality and habits. This seems to be important as a basis for a lasting relationship – although, of course, it is no guarantee.

V Composition

a) When choosing a partner for life, I do not think I would want my parents to be involved at the beginning because it should be the two of us who have to find out whether we can get on with each other or not. I would definitely want to enjoy that particular feeling you have when you have just fallen in love and I doubt that I would want to share this time with my parents.

But then, when we were both sure that this relationship could develop into something permanent, it would be important to me that my parents agreed with my choice as everything would be very complicated otherwise. I would also ask them for their opinion because, to quote Shakespeare, 'Love is blind' and it may sometimes be easier for somebody on the outside to spot possible problems.

I think that any potential conflict between my parents and me would also put a strain on the relationship with my partner. And I am convinced that if I felt that this was the real thing, my parents would share my view and welcome my partner into the family.

b) ME: Anne, you won't believe what's just happened.
ANNE: What? You're so pale. What's the matter?
ME: Robert's just phoned and told me that he'd spoken with his parents about the possibility of the two of us getting married and, guess what, they made a big fuss. They don't want us to get married!
ANNE: Oh, no. Why not?
ME: They say that we don't fit together. They say I come from a middle-class family ... as if I weren't worthy of their son.
ANNE: What a stupid thing to say.

145

ME: And they said that it's too soon for us to get married. First I should finish my degree and then we could still think about it. They think that we will have split up by then. But that won't happen, ever!

ANNE: What does Robert say?

ME: He's absolutely furious. He says that he shouldn't have to choose between his parents and me.

ANNE: I think everybody should cool down a bit and talk about it again in a few days. The two of you will find a solution. You'll have to find some sort of compromise because if you get married against his parents' wishes, your relationship will get really complicated.

ME: Yes, I know, you're right. I just won't mention it for a few days.

Notenschlüssel:

1	2	3	4	5	6
80–70	69–60	59–50	49–40	39–26	25–0

45 minutes

I   Listening comprehension: The Statue of Liberty (Track 7)

1. Complete the summary of the introduction.   (4 pts)

    This _____ is about American

    _____. This time, the subject is the

    Statue of Liberty, one of the world's most recognisable sights and

    the most well-known symbol of the United States of America.

2. Finish the sentences by ticking the correct statements.
    Several answers may be correct.   (8 pts)

    a) The first interviewee …

        ☐   is absolutely enthralled by the Statue of Liberty.

        ☐   is an engineer and therefore interested in the construc-
            tion.

        ☐   admires the determination of
            the creators of the statue.

        ☐   states that nobody had ever
            attempted to build anything
            on that scale before.

    b) The second interviewee …

        ☐   considers the statue to be a symbol
            of the Americans' pride in their
            country.

        ☐   arrived at Ellis Island as an
            immigrant.

        ☐   thinks that for immigrants the
            statue is a symbol of hope and a
            better life.

        ☐   hopes that America remains an
            immigrant nation.

3. Answer the following questions. You need not write in complete sentences. (10 pts)

   a) Which two Frenchmen built the Statue of Liberty?

   _____

   _____

   b) Who paid for the …

      statue? _____

      pedestal? _____

   c) How did the French raise the required money?

   _____

   _____

   _____

4. Decide whether the following statements are true or false. Correct the false statements. (12 pts)

		true	false

   a) With the construction of this statue, the French wanted to celebrate the French-American friend-ship and to create a symbol of liberty. ☐ ☐

   _____

   b) When they had the idea of the statue, they called it *Liberty Enlightening the United States*. ☐ ☐

   _____

   c) The statue represents the Roman goddess of justice, called Libertas. ☐ ☐

   _____

   d) The Statue of Liberty symbolised the promised land for those who were fleeing persecution and poverty. ☐ ☐

   _____

   _____

5. Complete the following text. (14 pts)

Well, after September 11th, the statue and Liberty Island were
_____ closed to the public. While
_____ reopened at the end of 2001, and
_____ was accessible again in August 2004,
the statue remained closed because, according to the National
Park Service, visitors could not safely be given access to the
statue since it would be too difficult to _____
it in case of _____. It was not reopened
to the public until May _____. And since then, only
a _____ number of people have been allowed to
climb up to the crown every day.

II Mediation (40 pts)

Your local adult educational centre is offering a series of lectures on
"American national symbols". When you find this leaflet, you show it
to Jamal, an Indian student who is staying with you for three months
in order to learn German. Since he is very interested in American culture as well, you think that this would be a good occasion to get a bit
of practice. His German is not very good yet, so you have to summarise the information for him in English and ask him which lecture he
would like to attend.

Write a dialogue in which you summarise the essential information
about the different national symbols and in which the two of you
agree on which lecture to attend.

Mount Rushmore

„Überwältigend, bewegend, einzigartig". Dies sind nur einige der Adjektive, mit denen die Besucher des *Mount Rushmore National Memorial* ihrer Begeisterung Ausdruck verleihen.

Der Referent an diesem Abend, Herr Samuel Müller, wird einen eindrucksvollen Einblick in die Entstehungsgeschichte und die Symbolik dieser Bergkette in den Black Hills in South Dakota vermitteln.

Die vier gigantischen Felsenporträts würdigen die amerikanischen Präsidenten, die zum Zeitpunkt der Entstehung des Denkmals als die bedeutendsten galten und damit die ersten 150 Jahre amerikanischer Geschichte repräsentieren. George Washington war der erste Präsident der USA. Thomas Jefferson erweiterte das Gebiet der USA beim sogenannten *Louisiana Purchase*. Theodore Roosevelt machte Amerika zu einer Weltmacht nicht zuletzt durch seinen Beitrag zur wirtschaftlichen Entwicklung. Und Abraham Lincoln einte das Land nach dem Bürgerkrieg.

Zwischen 1927 und 1941 meißelten der Bildhauer Gutzon Borglum und 400 Mitarbeiter die 18 Meter hohen Porträts aus dem Granit. Ursprünglich sollten sie nur mehr Touristen in die Region um die Black Hills locken, doch das Monument wurde zu einem amerikanischen Wahrzeichen, das überall auf der Welt bekannt ist.

Mount Rushmore National Memorial ist allerdings in seiner Entstehung nicht unumstritten, denn für die Lakota Indianer stellt das Monument eine Entweihung ihres heiligen Berges dar.

One World Trade Center

Niemand wird die Bilder jemals vergessen, die am 11. September 2001 um die Welt gingen: Die Zwillingstürme des World Trade Centers in Manhattan brechen nacheinander zusammen, nachdem zwei Passagierflugzeuge von Selbstmordattentätern hineingelenkt wurden. Zurück blieben die Trauer um mehr als 3 000 Opfer und eine offene Wunde mitten im Herzen der Stadt New York, der sogenannte Ground Zero.

Im zweiten Teil der Vortragsreihe über die nationalen Symbole Amerikas erläutert Prof. Dr. Dieter Dienstbier die Entstehung des One World Trade Center – umgangssprachlich auch als Freedom Tower bezeichnet – das genau an der Stelle in den Himmel ragt, wo die Türme einst standen.

Trotz anfänglicher Kontroversen, ob überhaupt und wenn ja, was gebaut werden sollte, entschied man sich schließlich dafür, hier einen Wolkenkratzer entstehen zu lassen, der mit 541,3 Metern Höhe zum Zeitpunkt der Fertigstellung zu den höchsten Bauwerken der Welt zählt und das höchste Gebäude in ganz Amerika ist. Zugleich gilt das Gebäude als eines der sichersten; es ist z. B. durch ein Betonfundament gegen Autobomben geschützt.

Der von Architekt David Childs entworfene World Trade Center Komplex umfasst außerdem noch drei weitere Bürogebäude sowie das National September 11 Memorial and Museum, ein Mahnmal für die Opfer der Terroranschläge am 11. September 2001 und der Bombenanschläge auf das WTC 1993.

Das Weiße Haus

Überall auf der Welt gilt es als Symbol für den Präsidenten der USA, für seine Regierung und für die USA selbst: das Weiße Haus.

Im dritten Teil der Vortragsreihe über die nationalen Symbole Amerikas führt Michael Schnitzler in die überaus interessante Geschichte des Weißen Hauses ein und illustriert das Leben in der Pennsylvania Avenue 1600 durch zahlreiche Anekdoten.

Das Weiße Haus ist seit mehr als 200 Jahren Amtssitz und offizielle Residenz des Präsidenten der Vereinigten Staaten von Amerika und seiner Familie.

Nachdem George Washington und der Stadtplaner Pierre L'Enfant den Ort ausgewählt hatten, wurde ein Wettbewerb ausgeschrieben, den der irische Architekt James Hoban gewann. Der Bau des von ihm entworfenen Gebäudes begann im Oktober 1792. Nach seiner Fertigstellung im Jahre 1800 wurde es von John Adams, dem zweiten Präsidenten der USA, erstmals bezogen. Seitdem hat jeder Präsident – und insbesondere jede First Lady – eigene Veränderungen vorgenommen und das Weiße Haus wurde nach und nach durch Anbauten vergrößert. Während der Amtszeit von Theodore Roosevelt wurde beispielsweise der Westflügel gebaut, da seine große Familie das Haupthaus bewohnte und so weitere Büroflächen notwendig wurden. Es war auch Theodore Roosevelt, der dem Haus aufgrund seines weißen Außenanstrichs offiziell seinen Namen gab. Präsident William H. Taft ließ 1909 das Präsidentenbüro umbauen und schuf das berühmte Oval Office im Westflügel.

Solution

The Statue of Liberty (Tapescript)

FEMALE ANNOUNCER: Welcome to today's radio program on American national symbols. Today, we will be talking about the Statue of Liberty, one of the world's most recognizable landmarks, the most universally recognized symbol of the United States. Our expert today is Doreen, a history student who works as a tour guide at the Statue of Liberty. But before we meet her, we want to know what Lady Liberty means to you. Let's listen to your thoughts.

MALE 1: It's impressive, isn't it? Whenever I see her, I'm absolutely amazed. It's an engineering marvel. I mean, just imagine how determined the engineers must have been to build this statue. It took more than twenty years to build the complete structure, I think. Before, nobody had ever tried to build anything near that size. I heard that they built the statue in France, dismantled it again in 350 pieces and shipped it to the United States. It's simply amazing that she is here, dominating the New York harbour.

MALE 2: Well, you know, it really makes me feel proud to be an American. It's a symbol. A symbol stands for an idea. And, I think, the Statue of Liberty is kind of a universal symbol of freedom. I always think of the pictures of people arriving at Ellis Island. The first thing they saw was the Statue of Liberty. Imagine this view. For millions of immigrants it was – and still is, I guess – the symbol of hope, of opportunity for those seeking a better life in America. And America as an immigrant nation really gave them the opportunity to provide a good life for themselves. So the lady with the crown definitely creates a sense of pride in our country. America is a great country.

FEMALE ANNOUNCER: Hello Doreen, you just heard that people are absolutely enthralled by the old lady here. What else can you tell us about the Statue of Liberty's beginnings here in America?

DOREEN: Well, some people think that the statue was a gift by the French government, but in fact it was the idea of a group of French individuals. The French sculptor Frédéric Auguste Bartholdi created the statue out of sheets of hammered copper, and the engineer Gustave Eiffel, who later designed the Eiffel Tower in Paris, was responsible for the statue's steel framework. As the construction would be really expensive, it was agreed that the French would finance the statue and the Americans would pay for the pedestal. On both sides, this required a big effort to raise the necessary funds, but the French were very inventive. They sold small models of the statue and tickets to view the construction activity. The French government even authorized a lottery.

FEMALE ANNOUNCER: It's incredible that people really made such a huge effort to create a really special gift to the United States. Could you explain to us why they were ready to invest so much money and time in this project?

DOREEN: The statue was conceived to celebrate French-American friendship and as a sign of their mutual desire for liberty. It was actually called *Liberty Enlightening the World* at the beginning. It represents Libertas, the Roman goddess of freedom. And, as you can see, Lady Liberty is stepping forward. This means that she is meant to be carrying the torch of liberty from the United States to the rest of the world. A nice idea, isn't it?

FEMALE ANNOUNCER: Yes, indeed. But nowadays, most Americans associate the statue with immigration. So why is that?

DOREEN: The statue took on a more universal meaning through time. From 1892 onwards, Ellis Island was a major port of entry for millions of European immigrants to the United States. The Statue of Liberty, the welcoming beacon, was the first thing they saw when arriving in New York by boat. And for those who wanted to escape persecution, oppression and poverty, looking for a better life, the Statue of Liberty was the symbol of the Promised Land. It represented hope and the possibility of a new beginning.

FEMALE ANNOUNCER: What happened in the aftermath of the September 11 attacks?

DOREEN: Well, after September 11, the statue and Liberty Island were immediately closed to the public. While the island reopened at the end of 2001, and the pedestal was accessible again in August 2004, the statue remained closed because, according to the National Park Service, visitors could not safely be given access to the statue since it would be too difficult to evacuate it in case of an emergency. It was not reopened to the public until May 2009. And since then, only a limited number of people have been allowed to climb up to the crown every day.

FEMALE ANNOUNCER: Doreen, thank you so much for your explanations. Enjoy your time here and good luck with your studies.

And for those of you who are interested in other national symbols of the United States, join us next week for our report on the national anthem "Star-Spangled Banner". Have a good week and thanks for listening.

I Listening comprehension

1. This **radio programme** is about American **national symbols**. This time, the subject is the Statue of Liberty, one of the world's most recognisable sights and the most well-known symbol of the United States of America.

2. a) The first interviewee …

   ☒ is absolutely enthralled by the Statue of Liberty.

   ☐ is an engineer and therefore interested in the construction.

   ☒ admires the determination of the creators of the statue.

   ☒ states that nobody had ever attempted to build anything on that scale before.

   b) The second interviewee …

   ☒ considers the statue to be a symbol of the Americans' pride in their country.

   ☐ arrived at Ellis Island as an immigrant.

   ☒ thinks that for immigrants the statue is a symbol of hope and a better life.

   ☐ hopes that America remains an immigrant nation.

3. a) The two men were F. A. Bartholdi and G. Eiffel.

   b) Who paid for the …

   statue? **the French**

   pedestal? **the Americans**

   c) The French sold small statues and tickets to see the construction site. They also had a lottery.

		true	false
4.	a) With the construction of this statue, the French wanted to celebrate the French-American friendship and to create a symbol of liberty.	☒	☐
	b) When they had the idea of the statue, they called it *Liberty Enlightening the* **World**.	☐	☒
	c) The statue represents the Roman goddess of **freedom**, called Libertas.	☐	☒
	d) The Statue of Liberty symbolised the promised land for those who were fleeing persecution and poverty.	☒	☐

155

5. Well, after September 11, the statue and Liberty Island were **immediately** closed to the public. While **the island** reopened at the end of 2001, and **the pedestal** was accessible again in August 2004, the statue remained closed because, according to the National Park Service, visitors could not safely be given access to the statue since it would be too difficult to **evacuate** it in case of **an emergency**. It was not reopened to the public until May **2009**. And since then, only a **limited** number of people have been allowed to climb up to the crown every day.

II Mediation

JAMAL: Oh, look at this. That is Mount Rushmore, isn't it? What does it say about it?

YOU: Yes, it is. The first lecture is about the Mount Rushmore National Memorial in the Black Hills in South Dakota. Do you know who they are? The four granite heads feature those American presidents who were considered to be the most important ones at the time the sculpture was created. So it's about the first 150 years of American history. Look, that's George Washington, the first American president. This one is Thomas Jefferson. It says here that he is portrayed because of the Louisiana Purchase. And, of course, Abraham Lincoln. He united the country after the Civil War. Well, I have to admit that I didn't know the fourth face. It's Theodore Roosevelt who advanced the economic development and made the United States a world power.

The sculptures were carved between 1927 and 1941. The sculptor's name was Gutzon Borglum. Originally, they only wanted to attract some more tourists to the Black Hills region. But, in fact, Mount Rushmore is controversial because for the Lakota Indians the monument desecrates their holy mountain. Sounds quite interesting, don't you think?

JAMAL: Wow, that sounds really interesting. Amazing what people can do when they are really convinced of an idea. What is the next one about? I've seen this picture before but I can't remember what it is now.

YOU: This is the One World Trade Center. You might have heard of it as the Freedom Tower. It's the skyscraper that is being built at Ground Zero, at the very place where the twin towers of the World Trade Center stood before the September 11 attacks. I remember that there was much debate about the future of Ground Zero. In the end, they decided to build this skyscraper. It says here that it is the tallest building in the United States and one of the tallest in the world. And it is one of the safest, of course. The new World Trade Center complex by David Childs features three more office buildings and the National September 11 Memorial and Museum, built to commemorate the victims of the terrorist attacks of both 2001 and 1993. I think I'd like to hear more about this.

JAMAL: Oh, I'd be really interested in that. But the next one is the White House. That's cool, too. What does it say here?

YOU: Well, it says that the White House has been the residence and the home of the President of the United States and his family for more than 200 years now. George Washington and the city planner Pierre L'Enfant chose the place and the Irish architect James Hoban designed the building. Construction started in October 1792. John Adams was the first to live in the White House in 1800. He was the second American President. Since then, every president and every first lady have added their own changes. Oh, here's an interesting example: Teddy Roosevelt had the West Wing built because he needed more space for offices since his large family lived in the main building. He also gave the White House its name because of its colour – I didn't know that, did you? And it was President Taft who had the Oval Office built in the West Wing in 1909.

JAMAL: To be honest, that one sounds a bit boring. All those presidents and dates. I'd prefer the lecture about the One World Trade Center.

YOU: Yeah, that's cool. Let's go to that one. It seems the most interesting to me, too.

Notenschlüssel:

1	2	3	4	5	6
88–77	76–66	65–55	54–44	43–29	28–0

60 minutes

Seeds of survival

The name alone makes it sound like a relict[1] from the Cold War or something out of a Bond film: it is referred to as the "Doomsday Vault[2]" and housed in an icy steel and concrete bunker, more than one hundred metres deep inside the mountain permafrost[3] of an Arctic archipelago[4]. Yet the Svalbard Global Seed
5 Vault is man's latest attempt to create a latter-day[5] Noah's Ark, or insurance policy, for the planet in the event of a catastrophe such as devastating climate change induced by global warming.

After decades of planning and construction work, the vault will officially start operating tomorrow. As the world's first global seed bank, it has the capacity to
10 hold up to 4.5 million batches of seeds from all the known varieties of the planet's main food crops.

The vault cost € 6 m to construct and has been built to withstand[6] nuclear missile attacks and even dramatic rises in sea levels that would result from both the Greenland and Antarctic ice shelves melting simultaneously.

15 The vault aims to make it possible to re-establish crops and plants should they disappear from their natural environment or be wiped out by major disasters. Cary Fowler, of the Global Crop Diversity Trust which set up the project together with Norway's Nordic Gene Bank yesterday described the vault as the "perfect place" for seed storage.

20 The vault is made up of three large, airtight, refrigerated cold-storage chambers which are housed in a long trident-shaped[7] tunnel bored through a layer of permafrost into a mountain of sandstone and limestone on the archipelago.

Norway's Svalbard's islands lie some 620 miles south of the North Pole deep inside the Arctic circle. No trees grow on the archipelago, which is home to some
25 2,300 people. It was selected because of its inhospitable[8] climate and remoteness[9]. The average winter temperature on Svalbard is around minus 14° C. The vault is protected by high walls of fortified concrete, doors armoured with steel plate and a home guard[10] of free-roaming polar bears.

"The facility is designed to hold twice as many varieties of agricultural crops as
30 we think exist," said Mr Fowler, "It will not be filled up in my lifetime nor in my grandchildren's lifetime, but at these temperatures, seeds for important crops like wheat, barley and peas can last for 1,000 years," he added.

The permafrost and rocks surrounding the tunnels are meant to ensure the seed samples remain frozen, even if the plant's refrigeration system fails and global

35 warming raises the outside temperature. "It is an insurance policy for the planet,"
Mr Carey said.

[…] [At] the project's inauguration[11], the vault will contain some 250,000 seed
samples.

Scientists involved in the project pointed out yesterday that some of the world's
40 biodiversity had already been lost as a result of war or natural disaster. Gene
vaults have disappeared in Iraq and Afghanistan following the US invasion and
seed banks in the Philippines and Honduras fell to natural disasters.

The Svalbard vault already appears to have survived its first environmental test.
Last Thursday what was described as "the biggest earthquake in Norway's his-
45 tory" – a tremor with a magnitude of 6.2 – was registered near the archipelago.

(531 words)

from "Norway's 'Doomsday Vault' holds seeds of survival" by Tony Paterson
http://www.independent.co.uk/news/world/europe/norways-doomsday-vault-holds-
seeds-of-survival-786773.html

Annotations
1 relict – sth. that has survived from an earlier time
2 vault – a room built for the safekeeping of sth. valuable
3 permafrost – a layer of soil that is always frozen in very cold regions of the world
4 archipelago – a large group of islands
5 latter-day – belonging to the present or recent times
6 to withstand – to resist
7 trident-shaped – in the form of a spear with three points on top
8 inhospitable – difficult to live in
9 remoteness – the state of being far away
10 home guard – a group of volunteers who want to defend their homeland; here: polar bears
  watching over the vault
11 inauguration – a formal beginning or introduction

I Multiple choice   (6 pts)

Tick the correct answer. Several answers may be correct.

1. The "Doomsday Vault" is …

    ☐ a relict of the Cold War.

    ☐ situated in a concrete bunker.

    ☐ buried under permafrost deep inside a mountain on an island.

    ☐ the successful attempt to rebuild Noah's Ark.

2. The Svalbard Global Seed Vault …

    ☐ is the world's first seed bank.

    ☐ is the first seed bank operating on a global scale.

    ☐ will hold seeds of all the main food crops.

    ☐ has been designed to hold 4.5 million different seeds.

3. The scientists who constructed the vault wanted it to …

    ☐ resist nuclear missile attacks.

    ☐ be independent from the general electricity supply.

    ☐ resist a potentially enormous rise in sea levels due to global warming.

    ☐ be situated between Greenland and the Arctic.

II Questions on the text   (40 pts)

1. Which objective did the scientists pursue when they built the Vault?

2. Why is the Vault situated on Norway's Svalbard's islands?

3. Why have some plants and seeds already disappeared?

III Diagram analysis and mediation   (20 pts)

This morning, you found the following diagram in your newspaper. As you have just read the article "Seeds of survival", you take the diagram with you to show to your English teacher. She is very pleased that you are taking such a great interest in the subject and asks you to present the diagram to your classmates the next day (in English of course).

Write about 200 words and present the diagram in the following way:
- Link it to the article "Seeds of survival".
- Present the facts and give short explanations for every point.

160

IV Comment   (30 pts)

Choose <u>one</u> of the following topics and write about 200 words.

1. Imagine you are the environment minister for one of the most important countries in the world. At an international conference on environmental pollution and destruction you are asked to give a speech about your environmental priorities.
    Explain which problems would be given top priority on your list and give reasons why.

2. What are the disadvantages of fossil fuels, nuclear power and renewable energies? Which would be the preferable energy source for the future? Discuss.

3. Do you think overpopulation is an important environmental issue? Justify your opinion.

Solution

Seeds of survival

I   Multiple choice

1. The "Doomsday Vault" is …

☐ a relict of the Cold War.

☒ situated in a concrete bunker.

☒ buried under permafrost deep inside a mountain on an island.

☐ the successful attempt to rebuild Noah's Ark.

2. The Svalbard Global Seed Vault …

☐ is the world's first seed bank.

☒ is the first seed bank operating on a global scale.

☒ will hold seeds of all the main food crops.

☒ has been designed to hold 4.5 million different seeds.

3. The scientists who constructed the vault wanted it to …

☒ resist nuclear missile attacks.

☐ be independent from the general electricity supply.

☒ resist a potentially enormous rise in sea levels due to global warming.

☐ be situated between Greenland and the Arctic.

II   Questions on the text

1. In the case of climate change brought about by global warming, some of the world's plants could disappear so scientists are trying to preserve the earth's biodiversity and especially all the known food crops by storing their seeds in the vault. With the help of these seeds it will be possible to ensure their further existence.

2. Norway's Svalbard's islands have been chosen as the ideal place for the vault because of their arctic climate and the fact that they are far away from civilisation. The extremely cold temperatures, the frozen ground and the rocks around the vault ensure that the seeds will be protected even if global warming causes the average temperature to rise.

3. Some plants and seeds have already disappeared due to war and natural disasters. In addition to that, other seed banks have been destroyed in armed conflicts or as a result of natural disasters.

III Diagram analysis and mediation

Hinweis: Bei dieser Aufgabe sollst du eine Grafik aus einer deutschen Zeitung auf Englisch präsentieren. Dabei gibt es Folgendes zu beachten: Laut Aufgabenstellung sollst du die Grafik mit dem vorangehenden Artikel „Seeds of Survival" in Verbindung bringen und darüber hinaus für jeden der genannten Punkte eine kurze Erklärung geben. Die Verknüpfung zu dem Artikel lässt sich am einfachsten in ein oder zwei einleitenden Sätzen herstellen, die dann zum Thema der Grafik überleiten. Für die in der Grafik genannten Punkte gilt es dann, eine kurze Erklärung zu finden. Greife auf dein Weltwissen und auf das zurück, was ihr bereits im Unterricht besprochen habt. Um eine kurze Erläuterung zu geben, können dir folgende Fragestellungen helfen: Woran liegt es? Was werden die Konsequenzen sein? Wer ist verantwortlich? Es reicht völlig aus, die genannten Tatsachen mit einem oder zwei Sätzen plausibel zu erklären. Die folgenden Erklärungen sind ein Lösungsvorschlag, selbstverständlich kannst du auch andere Aspekte in den Mittelpunkt stellen.

The Svalbard Global Seed Vault was constructed because the world's biodiversity is threatened with extinction if global warming causes more natural disasters and a general rise in temperature. That this was necessary is shown by this diagram, which illustrates how much of our environment is destroyed every single day.

Every single day, more than 70 animal and plant species die out because of environmental changes and the growing human population needing more space.

Every single day, 253 000 tonnes of fish are caught, which may result in the extinction of some species and in the risk of losing a valuable food source which many people depend upon, especially in poorer countries.

Every single day, the arable farmland is reduced by 27 000 hectares, which implies that the possibilities for growing crops are further restricted, especially in poorer countries.

Every single day, 26 000 hectares of tropical rainforest are destroyed because, for example, the space is needed to grow the crops for bio fuel.

Every single day, 65 million tonnes of carbon dioxide are released into the atmosphere, and so far most countries have not been able to reduce the carbon dioxide emissions effectively – the industrialised countries do not want to see their wealth at risk and the poorer countries struggle to reach a better standard of living.

And every single day, 9.1 billion cubic metres of fresh water are consumed worldwide. Will there be enough for more than seven billion people on earth?

IV Comment

1. In the 21st century we have to face an increasing number of severe environmental problems caused mainly by ourselves.

    Our primary concern at the moment is air contamination caused by polluting industries and traffic. Attempts to deal with carbon dioxide emissions (the main pollutant) on a global scale have not been very successful so far. Of course, industry will have to look for more environmentally friendly methods of production – and our government will see to it that they find efficient solutions. But I think this is a problem where every single one of us can start to make a difference: you have the choice whether to take the car to drive down to the next supermarket or to go by bike. That is why air pollution is top on our list of environmental problems.

    Next on the list is water pollution. Factories release toxic waste into our rivers and oceans. Pesticides and fertilisers contribute further to water contamination. Oil spills caused by damaged oil rigs and oil tankers have recently raised public awareness of the fact that we do not really value our most important resource. We have to remind people how valuable water is since it is likely to become scarce one day. That is why water pollution is next on our list.

    These are only two of the various problems we are facing. And since environmental problems do not stop at national borders, we can only tackle them by cooperating with each other.

2. Today, there are many different ways to produce energy. We can use fossil fuels like coal, oil and gas, nuclear power, or renewable energy sources such as the sun, wind and water. But all of these energy sources have disadvantages, so it is difficult to decide which to choose.

    One of the main disadvantages of using fossil fuels is that the supplies will disappear in the foreseeable future. Another negative aspect is certainly that burning fossil fuels causes severe environmental problems, like acid rain and global warming.

    Nuclear power, however, does not seem to be a good alternative to fossil fuels. Although the immediate effects on the environment may not be as serious, in the long run, radioactive waste has to be disposed of safely, which is a problem for which we have no solution as yet. In addition, even experts do not seem to be able to predict the long-term effects that radiation from nuclear power plants has on human beings and the environment. They are not able to prevent serious accidents either, like the one in Japan.

    One of the disadvantages of renewable energy sources is that it is difficult to reliably generate the quantities of electricity needed in industrialised countries because the process often depends on the weather conditions. In addition to that, renewable energy technology is much more expensive – at least at the moment.

In conclusion, it seems best to rely on renewable energy sources because the disadvantages of fossil fuels and nuclear power do not apply to them. At the same time, people should try to reduce the amount of energy they use.

3. Some time ago, the media announced the birth of the seven billionth person. Several children around the world were welcomed by the United Nations and chosen to symbolically represent this population milestone. But, in fact, this is not a cause for celebration since overpopulation is one of the most important, if not the most important environmental issue.

The increase in human population has an impact on all the other environmental problems we have to face today: forests are cut down in order to obtain land for farming and housing and timber for construction. This, in turn, affects animal and plant species that are displaced or even become extinct.

Furthermore, there is an increased demand for natural resources, of course. Mankind is using up natural resources like fresh water or fossil fuels at an alarming rate, i.e. faster than the rate of regeneration. In many areas, there is not enough food to feed the growing population.

More people also means that more carbon dioxide is released into the atmosphere. Densely populated countries such as China are struggling to improve their standard of living and to close the gap on the industrialised countries. This implies that more people use automobiles, for example, so that more fuel is required and more pollution is caused.

Overpopulation might not be the cause of our environmental problems but it aggravates the situation perceptibly. Thus, it seems that limiting birth rates through increased access to birth control and contraception, for example, might be one of the steps that could be taken to conserve our environment.

Notenschlüssel:

1	2	3	4	5	6
96–84	83–72	71–60	59–48	47–32	31–0

45 minutes

Extract from *Nice Work*

Robyn Penrose, a university lecturer specialising in feminist theory and the 19th cen-
tury English industrial novel, is visiting an engineering firm run by Vic Wilcox. Both
of them take part in an exchange programme between academics and industrialists.

The machine shop was an enormous shed with machines and work benches laid
out in a grid pattern. Wilcox led her down the broad central aisle[1], with occasion-
al detours[2] to left and right to point out some particular operation. Robyn soon
gave up trying to follow his explanations. She could hardly hear them because of
5 the din[3], and the few words and phrases that she did catch – "tolerances to five
thou", "cross-boring", "CNC machine", "index round" – meant nothing to her.
The machines were ugly, filthy[4] and surprisingly old-fashioned in appearance.
The typical operation seemed to be that the man took a lump of metal from a bin,
thrust it into the machine, closed some kind of safety cage, and pulled a lever.
10 Then he opened the cage, took out the part (which now looked slightly different)
and dropped it into another bin. He did all this as noisily as possible.
"Does he do the same thing all day?" she shouted at Wilcox, after they had
watched one such man at work for some minutes. He nodded. "It seems terribly
monotonous. Couldn't it be done automatically?"
15 Wilcox led her to a slightly quieter part of the shop floor. "If we had the capital
to invest in new machines, yes. And if we cut down the number of our operations
– for the part he's making it wouldn't be worth automating. The quantities are too
small."
"Couldn't you move him to another job occasionally[5]?" she said, with a sudden
20 burst of inspiration. "Move them all about, every few hours, just to give them a
change?" […]
"They don't like being shunted[6] about. You start moving men about from one
job to another, and they start complaining, or demanding to be put on a higher
grade. Not to mention the time lost changing over."
25 "So it comes back to money again."
"Everything does, in my experience."
"Never mind what the men want?"
"They prefer it this way, I'm telling you. They switch off, they daydream. If they
were smart enough to get bored, they wouldn't be doing a job like this in the first
30 place. […] There you are," said Wilcox. "Our one and only CNC machine."
"What?"

"Computer-numerically controlled machine. See how quickly it changes tools?"
Robyn peered though a Perspex window and watched things moving round and
going in and out in sudden spasms, lubricated[7] by spurts of a liquid that looked
35 like milky coffee.

"What's it doing?"

"Machining cylinder heads. Beautiful, isn't it?

"Not the word I'd choose." [...]

"One day," said Wilcox, "there will be lightless factories full of machines like
40 that." [...]

"And the Managing Director? Will he be a computer too, sitting in a dark office?"

Wilcox considered the question seriously. "No, computers can't think. There'll
always have to be a man in charge, at least one man, deciding what should be
45 made, and how. But these jobs" – he jerked his head round at the rows of benches
– "will no longer exist. This machine here is doing the work that was done last
year by twelve men."

"O brave new world," said Robyn, "where only the managing directors have
jobs."
50 This time Wilcox did not miss her irony. "I don't like making men redundant[8],"
he said, "but we're caught in a double bind[9]. If we don't modernise we lose competitive edge[10] and have to make men redundant, and if we *do* modernise we
have to make men redundant because we don't need 'em any more. [...] Men
like to work. It's a funny thing, but they do. They may moan about it every Mon-
55 day morning, they may agitate for shorter hours and longer holidays, but they
need to work for their self-respect."

"That's just conditioning. People could get used to life without work."

"Could *you*? I thought you enjoyed your work."

"That's different."
60 "Why?"

"Well, it's nice work. It's meaningful. It's rewarding[11]. I don't mean in money
terms. It would be worth doing even if one wasn't paid anything at all. And the
conditions are decent – not like this." She swept her arm round in a gesture that
embraced the oil-laden atmosphere, the roar of machinery, the crash of metal, the
65 whine[12] of electric trolleys, the worn, soiled ugliness of everything. [...]

(704 words)

from "Nice Work" by David Lodge. London: Secker & Warburg, 1988.

Annotations
1 aisle – a passageway between rows of seats, shelves or machines
2 detour – a long or roundabout route taken to avoid sth. or to make a visit along the way
3 din – a loud, unpleasant, continuous noise
4 filthy – very dirty
5 occasionally – from time to time
6 to shunt – here: to transfer from one place to another

7   to lubricate – to cover with an oily substance in order to lessen friction
8   to make s.o. redundant – to dismiss s.o. as being no longer needed for work
9   to be caught in a double bind – to be in a difficulty which cannot be solved in an easy or pleasant way
10 to lose competitive edge – to risk being no longer as good as, or even better than others
11 rewarding – giving personal satisfaction
12 whine – a continuous high-pitched sound

I   Working with the text   (40 pts)

Read all the questions first. Then answer them in the given order.
Use your own words as far as appropriate.

1.   Contrast Robyn's and Vic's attitudes towards what they see in the machine shop and towards the men's working conditions.

2.   Illustrate Robyn's and Vic's perceptions of the "CNC machine" (l. 30).

3.   Explain the dilemma Vic is in. What does this have to do with the workers' "self-respect" (l. 56)?

II   Composition   (30 pts)

In search of a summer job in an English-speaking country, 17-year-old Johanna Meier from Coburg finds the following job offer online. Write a convincing letter of application for her which shows that she fulfils all the qualifications. (You need not write a complete curriculum vitae, but you should refer to it in your letter.)

We are currently looking to recruit a

German-Speaking Exhibition Assistant
for our special exhibition on Prince Albert and Queen Victoria
and their relations with Germany.

The exhibition will take place from July 1st to September 30th in London.
We would be glad to have a German native speaker join our team.

Key Responsibilities
• Meet and greet all visitors
• Offer guided tours of the exhibition in German
• Deal with telephone enquiries from journalists, exhibitors and visitors
• Update websites
• Proof-read exhibition leaflet and press documents in English and German

Skills, Knowledge, Experience
• Fluent written and spoken German is required, with excellent English
• Strong interpersonal and organisational skills
• Computer literacy, including knowledge of Word, Excel and HTLM

If you are at least 16 years old and interested in this job, please email
your letter of application with a C.V. to:
princealbertexhibition@thelondonmuseums.co.uk

Solution

Extract from *Nice Work*

I   Working with the text

1. Robyn Penrose, probably visiting the factory for the first time, finds the machines ugly and dirty. She is concerned about the boring and repetitive work and thinks about ways and methods to make the men's work more bearable.

   Vic Wilcox, however, is obviously very proud of his factory's machine shop. He rejects any suggestion of improvement because he is primarily interested in the highest possible profit for his factory. Replacing the workers with a machine would not be worth it because of the small quantities involved. He doesn't see any necessity to move the workers to different machines; he even says that the men prefer it the way it is.

2. When Vic and Robyn reach the place where the CNC machine, the computer-numerically controlled machine, is working, Vic presents it lovingly as "[o]ur one and only CNC machine" (l. 30) and describes it as "beautiful" (l. 37), as if it were a human being. He is very proud of the CNC machine, which is much quicker and more efficient than men.

   At first, Robyn does not really know what he is talking about because she only sees "things moving round and going in and out in sudden spasms" (ll. 33/34). She does not share Vic's enthusiasm for the machine but is simply appalled by the idea that these machines might take the place of human workers.

3. In the course of the conversation, Vic explains the difficulty he is confronted with concerning modernisation. He says that if they did not use the latest machines, they would not be able to compete with other factories and thus be forced to dismiss workers. On the other hand, if they modernised, the workers would become superfluous anyway because the work would be done by machines. And he is aware of the fact that work is important for people's "self-respect" (l. 56). But only minutes before he says that he would be prepared to fire people in order to increase the factory's competitiveness and profitability, so his concern for the workers does not really seem to be genuine.

II Composition

Dear Sir/Madam

I am writing in reference to your job offer for a German-speaking exhibition
assistant. I am 17 years old and I live in Coburg, Prince Albert's birthplace. I
have always been interested in the history of my hometown and thus I am confident that my knowledge of Coburg's ducal family will help me to offer qualified guided tours of your exhibition in German.

I am particularly attracted to your job because I would love to spend the summer
in London, where I will have the opportunity to improve my language skills
further. German is my native language and, after seven years of English at
school, I have a very good command of the English language, both written and
spoken. I am also computer literate (Word, Excel and PowerPoint) and able to
update websites.

As you can see from my enclosed curriculum vitae, I have been a member of the
local group of Girl Guides since I was eight years old. As a group leader, I am
responsible for organising trips and exchange programmes. This experience and
the fact that I am a very open-minded and outgoing person will help me deal
with all the people interested in the exhibition.

I believe that I could be an asset to your team and look forward to hearing from
you soon.

Yours faithfully
Johanna Meier

Encl.

Notenschlüssel:

1	2	3	4	5	6
70–62	61–53	52–44	43–35	34–23	22–0

170

45 minutes

Extract from *Looks and Smiles*

Mick has just finished school and is looking for a job. He lives with his parents in Sheffield in the early '80s, when Britain suffered a severe recession and unemployment reached record levels.

Mrs Reid looked up and turned her chair towards him.

"Now then, Michael, it says here that you'd like to be a motor mechanic, or go into engineering. Something like that."

Mick laughed and Mrs Reid was so surprised by his response that she checked
5 his card to make sure that she had read it correctly.

"What are you laughing at?"

"It always makes me laugh when somebody calls me Michael. It sounds as though they're talking to somebody else."

"Why, what do people usually call you?"

10 "You'd be surprised."

"When they're being polite, that is."

"Mick."

"Right, Mick. Have you started looking for jobs yet?"

"Course I have. I look in the paper every day. I've written in for some jobs as
15 well."

"Have you had any replies yet?"

"I've had a couple saying they've no vacancies."

"So you haven't been for any interviews yet, then?"

Mick shook his head, but not slowly in a despondent[1] manner.

20 "No, not yet. But I should get something, though. I've written in to stacks of places." […]

"Well, I'm afraid we've nothing in your line at the moment, Mick. There are lots of boys after craft[2] apprenticeships but unfortunately there's not many firms taking them on just now."

25 She picked up a small pile of 'jobs vacant' cards from her desk.

"I don't suppose you'd be willing to consider anything else at this stage?"

"Like what?"

Mick watched her look through the cards. She knew their details as intimately as a little boy his footballers.

30 "Well, there's a vacancy here for a junior in a warehouse …"

She made a tough face and continued to read from the card in a deeper, more masculine voice,

"… Strong, fit lad essential."

And as she catalogued these athletic requirements she flexed one arm in a parody
35 of a strong man. Mick could not tell whether she was suggesting the job seriously, or just ridiculing the advertisement.

"What would I be doing?"

Mrs Reid became herself again.

"You'd be unloading lorries and carrying stuff about, furniture and things like
40 that."

"You what! I'm not doing that! I want a trade. What's the point in taking exams and getting qualifications and then going into a dead-end³ job like that? It's a waste of time, isn't it?"

Mrs Reid smiled and nodded sympathetically. She heard the same story a dozen
45 times a day. But she did not have the heart to discourage him. He had only just left school. His working life had only just begun.

"Well, we've got a note here of what you have in mind, Mick. If anything comes in and we think you might be suitable, we'll be in touch. In the meantime, don't just rely on us to find you a job. Something usually turns up if you try hard
50 enough. Now then …"

She took a blank appointment card off a thick pile and began to fill it in. […]

"This is your appointment card. You take this up to the Social Security office and sign on at the time it says here." She pointed out the time in the appropriate box. "That's ten-thirty every other Wednesday. Have you got that?"

55 Mick read the details and nodded.

"If you don't, your Giro⁴ won't come through, so don't forget."

Mick stood up and walked across the room. When he reached the door, Mrs Reid said: "Good luck, Mick."

Mick turned and smiled at her, then went out.

60 As soon as he had gone, she abandoned all pretence of optimism and just sat there for a few seconds staring at the wall. But there was no time to be depressed. Not here anyway. There were other boys and girls to see: dozens of them, today, tomorrow, next week.

She stood up and crossed the room, and when she called the next boy in, she
65 managed to greet him with a smile too. […]   *(650 words)*

Barry Hines, "Looks and Smiles". London: Joseph, 1981.

Annotations
1 despondent – feeling or showing extreme discouragement and depression
2 craft – a trade or occupation requiring special (especially manual) skill
3 dead-end – not leading any further; lacking opportunities
4 Giro – a cheque given by the British government to someone who is unemployed

I Working with the text (40 pts)

1. Characterise Mick.

2. Examine Mrs Reid's relationship with her job.

II Indirect speech (20 pts)

The next day, Mick tells his best friend Alan about the conversation with Mrs Reid.

Use indirect speech to report what Mrs Reid and Mick said. Use different introductory verbs in the past tense. Mind the correct pronouns.

Well, when I came into her office, she called me Michael and I had to laugh. She _____

("What are you laughing at?" l. 6) and I _____

_____ ("It always

makes me laugh when somebody calls me Michael." l. 7) and so I told her that I preferred to be called Mick.

Then she _____

("Have you started looking for jobs yet?" l. 13) and I _____

_____

_____ ("I look in the paper every day. I've written in

for some jobs as well." ll. 14/15) but, obviously, I haven't had any luck yet.

As they didn't have anything in my line, she _____

_____

("I don't suppose you'd be willing to consider anything else at this stage?" l. 26) but nevertheless she suggested a job as a warehouse assistant. But of course I didn't want that kind of dead-end job.

So the lady finally said that if _____

("If anything comes in and we think you might be suitable, we'll be in touch." ll. 47/48.) and she _____

_____

("don't just rely on us to find you a job." ll. 48/49). And then she wished me good luck. Well, I will need that because I don't think that they will get me a job. I'll have to do it on my own.

173

III Cartoon analysis (30 pts)

Describe this cartoon and explain the irony.
Contrast it to Mick's story above.

"I'm sorry, Mr. Naheed, we have no openings for you.
All of those jobs were outsourced to your home country."

© Dale Wilkins

Solution

Extract from *Looks and Smiles*

I   Working with the text

> *Hinweis: Bei diesem Text sollst du zunächst den Protagonisten Mick charakterisieren und anschließend Mrs Reids Verhältnis zu ihrem Job. Bei solchen Aufgabenstellungen ist es wichtig, dass du deine Feststellungen durch Textstellen belegst. Vergiss also nicht in Klammern auf entsprechende Zeilen im Text zu verweisen. Du kannst natürlich auch mit Zitaten arbeiten.*

1. Mick has just left school (cf. ll. 45/46), so he should be about 16 years old. He is quite self-confident for a person that age. He appears at Mrs Reid's office looking for a job and his first reaction, when she calls him Michael, is to laugh (cf. l. 4). Perhaps he is a bit nervous in this situation but he explains rather straightforwardly that he is usually called Mick (cf. l. 12), which might not be completely suitable considering the situation.

   He is a very serious young man who really wants to find a job. He seems a bit annoyed when Mrs Reid asks him whether he has already started looking for a job (cf. ll. 14/15). To him this might sound as if Mrs Reid was implying that he was not really making an effort, which is definitely not the case.

   Mick is an optimistic boy. Although he has not been lucky so far, he is not discouraged (cf. l. 19) and is positive about finding something (cf. l. 20).

   He is also aware of his skills and his qualifications because he is looking for a position as a motor mechanic or in engineering and does not accept a job as a junior in a warehouse because this would lead him nowhere (cf. ll. 41/42). So he is quite intelligent, too.

2. Mrs Reid's job is to talk to the young people who are looking for jobs, to find them a position if possible and to give them their appointment cards if there is nothing for them so that they can at least claim unemployment benefit.

   She takes her job very seriously and would really like to help the young people that come to her office. She makes time for Mick (cf. ll. 4–13) and is well prepared (cf. ll. 28/29).

   She apologises for not having anything for Mick at the moment (cf. l. 22), but in order not to discourage him completely she proposes a different job as a warehouse assistant (cf. l. 30). Although she knows that Mick is overqualified for this work, she tries to interest him in the job by alluding to his obvious physical abilities (cf. ll. 34/35). Even though she knows that there will not be any job available for Mick any time soon (cf. l. 45) she insists on him continuing to look for a job on his own (cf. ll. 48–50).

175

For her, Mick is only one of dozens of young people that she has to see every day. And for everyone it is the same – no jobs available. Obviously, Mrs Reid feels sorry for them (cf. l. 45 and l. 61) and is aware of how bad the situation is (cf. l. 62). However, since she does not want them to lose hope, she pretends to be optimistic (cf. l. 61) and manages to smile at every one of them and treat them all in a friendly way (cf. l. 65) because it is her job to do so.

II   Indirect speech

Hinweis: Möchte man betonen, dass etwas immer noch so ist wie zur Zeit des ursprünglichen Gesprächs oder handelt es sich bei dem Gesagten um eine universelle Wahrheit (Bsp. "My teacher explained that oil is lighter than water."), dann kann auch in der indirekten Rede mit einem einleitenden Verb in einer Vergangenheitsform das Präsens stehen. Auch hier ist es jedoch möglich, die Zeitform anzupassen („backshift").

Well, when I came into her office, she called me Michael and I had to laugh. She **wanted to know what I was laughing at** and I **explained to her that it always made/makes me laugh when somebody called/calls me Michael** and so I told her that I preferred to be called Mick.

Then she **asked me if/whether I had started looking for jobs yet** and **I answered that I looked/look in the paper every day and that I had/have written in for some jobs as well** but, obviously, I haven't had any luck yet.

As they didn't have anything in my line, she **said that she didn't suppose that I'd be willing to consider anything else at that stage** but nevertheless she suggested a job as a warehouse assistant. But of course I didn't want that kind of dead-end job.

So the lady finally said that if **anything came in and they thought I might be suitable, they would be in touch** and she **told me not to just rely on them to find me a job**. And then she wished me good luck. Well, I will need that because I don't think that they will get me a job. I'll have to do it on my own.

III   Cartoon analysis

The cartoon shows two men in an office.

One of them is seen from behind. He is almost bald and is wearing glasses and what seems to be a suit and shirt. He is sitting at a desk, holding a piece of paper which is probably a cover letter or a curriculum vitae of the man opposite.

The second man, who is sitting in front of the desk, is also wearing a suit with a shirt and tie. He has got dark skin; it is very likely that he is from India, Pakistan or Bangladesh.

176

The older man addresses him as "Mr. Naheed". Mr. Naheed is looking quite concerned because the older man says to him, "I'm sorry, Mr. Naheed, we have no openings for you. All of those jobs were outsourced to your home country."

The irony of this situation is that Mr. Naheed very likely came to the place where he is now because he was looking for a better job and a better life than in his own country. But now, he does not get a job (for which he is obviously qualified) since the kind of occupation he was after has been transferred to his home country – probably because the workers there are cheaper.

Mick's story takes place in the early '80s, so the reason why he does not find a job cannot be attributed to outsourcing, which is quite a recent phenomenon in the context of globalisation, but rather to the social and economic situation in England at that time.

Notenschlüssel:

1	2	3	4	5	6
90–79	78–67	66–56	55–45	44–30	29–0

45 minutes

English won't dominate as world language

More bilingual people expected in future, expert says

WASHINGTON – The world faces a future of people speaking more than one language, with English no longer seen as likely to become dominant, a British language expert says in a new analysis.

"English is likely to remain one of the world's most important languages for the
5 foreseeable future, but its future is more problematic – and complex – than most people appreciate," said language researcher David Graddol.

He sees English as likely to become the "first among equals" rather than having the global field to itself.

"Monolingual speakers of any variety of English – American or British – will
10 experience increasing difficulty in employment and political life, and are likely to become bewildered[1] by many aspects of society and culture around them," Graddol said.

The share of the world's population that speaks English as a native language is falling, Graddol reports […].

15 The idea of English becoming the world language to the exclusion of others "is past its sell-by date[2]," Graddol says. Instead, its major contribution will be in creating new generations of bilingual and multilingual speakers, he reports.

Multi-lingual homes

A multi-lingual population is already the case in much of the world and is be-
20 coming more common in the United States. Indeed, the Census Bureau reported last year that nearly one American in five speaks a language other than English at home, with Spanish leading, and Chinese growing fast.

[…]

Yale linguist Stephen Anderson noted that multilingualism is "more or less the
25 natural state. In most of the world multilingualism is the normal condition of people."

"The notion[3] that English shouldn't, needn't and probably won't displace[4] local languages seems natural to me," he said in a telephone interview.

While it is important to learn English, he added, politicians and educators need to
30 realize that doesn't mean abandoning the native language.

Graddol […] anticipates a world where the share of people who are native English speakers slips from 9 percent in the mid-twentieth century to 5 percent in 2050.

Chinese in the lead

35 As of 1995, he reports, English was the second most-common native tongue in the world, trailing only Chinese.

By 2050, he says, Chinese will continue its predominance, with Hindi-Urdu of India and Arabic climbing past English, and Spanish nearly equal to it.

Swarthmore College linguist K. David Harrison noted, however, that "the global
40 share of English is much larger if you count second-language speakers, and will continue to rise, even as the proportion of native speakers declines."

[…]

Even as it grows as a second language, English may still not ever be the most widely spoken language in the world, according to Graddol, since so many
45 people are native Chinese speakers and many more are learning it as a second language.

[…]

More languages on the web

[…] [I]n the early years of the Internet it was dominated by sites in English, but
50 in recent years there has been a proliferation of non-English sites, especially Spanish, German, French, Japanese and others.

Nonetheless, English is strong as a second language, and teaching it has become a growth industry, said Montgomery, a Seattle-based geologist and energy consultant. Graddol noted, though that employers in parts of Asia are already
55 looking beyond English. "In the next decade the new 'must learn' language is likely to be Mandarin."

"The world's language system, having evolved over centuries, has reached a point of crisis and is rapidly restructuring," Graddol says. In this process as many as 90 percent of the 6,000 or so languages spoken around the world may
60 be doomed to extinction, he estimated.

[…]   *(587 words)*

© *AP/dapd*

Annotations
1   bewildered – confused
2   sell-by date – the date stamped on food products indicating the day by which they should be sold
3   notion – idea, conception
4   to displace – to cause sth. to move from its usual position

I Paraphrases

(10 pts)

Paraphrase the underlined parts of the following sentences.

1. "educators need to realize that doesn't mean <u>abandoning</u> the native language" (ll. 29/30)

   _____

2. "Graddol […] <u>anticipates</u> a world where the share of people who are native English speakers <u>slips</u> from 9 percent in the mid-twentieth century to 5 percent in 2050." (ll. 31–33)

   _____

   _____

3. "English was the second most-common native tongue in the world, <u>trailing only</u> Chinese." (ll. 35/36)

   _____

4. "but in recent years there has been a <u>proliferation</u> of non-English sites" (ll. 49/50)

   _____

II Working with the text

(50 pts)

Read all the questions first. Then answer them in the given order. Use your own words as far as appropriate.

1. What does David Graddol mean when he sees English as the "first among equals" (l. 7) in the future? What does this imply for people who only speak English?

2. Which role will the English language play?

3. How is the world's language system being restructured at the moment?

III Translation (30 pts)

Translate the newspaper clipping "The Web in Chinese" into good, idiomatic German.

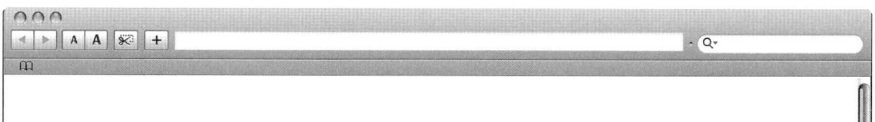

The Web in Chinese?

With the Internet being an American invention, it seems to be obvious that the dominant language on the Net is English. But several studies show that, in the last few years, the English language has lost its pre-eminent position because of the increasing number of non-English speakers who publish websites and search for content in their own languages. Among the top ten languages on the Internet are Spanish, Portuguese, German, Arabic and Japanese, but the language that is likely to replace English as the most popular language on the Internet in the near future is Chinese. While the English language is spoken by more than 500 million people as their first or second language, Chinese has over double that amount of speakers, yet fewer of them have access to the Internet. But since China's economic power has been increasing at an unprecedented rate recently, the Chinese's living standard has also been improving considerably. So the Chinese language has an enormous potential to expand through the Internet.

Solution

English won't dominate as world language

Hinweis: *Dieser Text ist anspruchsvoll. Nimm dir deshalb genügend Zeit, ihn sorgfältig zu lesen, bis du verstanden hast, worum es geht. Achte auch darauf, dass es an einigen Stellen um die Personen, deren Muttersprache Englisch ist, und an anderen Stellen um die Menschen, die insgesamt Englisch sprechen (also auch als Fremdsprache), geht.*

I Paraphrases

1. completely giving up

2. predicts/expects
   declines/decreases

3. only following behind Chinese

4. a rapid increase in the number

II Working with the text

1. The English language seemed on its way to becoming the world's most important language. But in his new analysis, David Graddol explains that English will probably only be the "first among equals", i.e. there will be several languages of equal importance. Even if we take the second-language speakers into account it may not be the most widespread language in the future since there are so many native Chinese speakers and many people learn Mandarin as a second language as well.
   For monolingual English speakers this will imply that it will be far more difficult for them to get a job and to understand the world surrounding them concerning political, cultural and social aspects in general.

2. The English language will remain important, but people will learn it in addition to their native language instead of replacing it. Thus, more people will be bilingual and multilingual.
   In addition, the number of English native speakers will decrease. According to Graddol, English will probably never top Chinese as the most widely spoken language in the world.

3. So far, a lot of people have been learning English as a second language because it was a necessity, for example, in a job. But now, employers are already looking for people speaking Chinese, as this is likely to become the universal means of communication in the future.

This development might result in the extinction of a large number of the over 6,000 other languages spoken worldwide.

III Translation

Hinweis: Hier handelt es sich um eine „echte" Übersetzung, nicht um eine Mediation. Lies dir den Text zunächst durch, bis du verstanden hast, worum es geht. Dann übersetze Satz für Satz ins Deutsche. Wenn du fertig bist, lies dir den deutschen Text noch einmal durch, ohne die englische Vorlage hinzuzuziehen. Klingt er wirklich wie ein deutscher Text oder wie eine Übersetzung? Vielleicht kannst du noch das eine oder andere verbessern.

Das Internet auf Chinesisch?

Das Internet ist eine amerikanische Erfindung, daher scheint es offensichtlich, dass Englisch die im Netz vorherrschende Sprache ist. Doch mehrere Studien zeigen, dass die englische Sprache in den letzten Jahren ihre Vorrangstellung verloren hat, da die Zahl der Nutzer steigt, die kein Englisch sprechen und in ihrer eigenen Sprache Websites veröffentlichen und nach Inhalten suchen. Zu den zehn meist verwendeten Sprachen im Internet gehören Spanisch, Portugiesisch, Deutsch, Arabisch und Japanisch, doch die Sprache, die Englisch in naher Zukunft wahrscheinlich als beliebteste Sprache im Internet ablösen wird, ist Chinesisch.

Während Englisch von mehr als 500 Millionen Menschen als Erst- oder Zweitsprache gesprochen wird, gibt es mehr als doppelt so viele Personen, die Chinesisch sprechen, allerdings haben weniger von ihnen Zugang zum Internet. Da aber Chinas Wirtschaftsmacht in letzter Zeit so stark zugenommen hat, wie noch nie zuvor, hat sich auch der Lebensstandard der Chinesen erheblich verbessert. Aus diesem Grund hat die chinesische Sprache gewaltiges Potential, sich über das Internet zu verbreiten.

Notenschlüssel:

1	2	3	4	5	6
90–79	78–67	66–56	55–45	44–30	29–0

45 minutes

Großbritanniens Überwachungssystem ist gescheitert

Seit Jahren setzen London und andere britische Städte auf eine großflächige Kameraüberwachung. Die Krawalle zeigen, wie unzulänglich diese Technik ist.

Tausende von Kameras stehen auf den Straßen von London und anderer britischer Städte. Sie alle sahen zu als in den vergangenen Tagen Jugendliche gegen die Polizei kämpften, Stadtviertel in Schutt und Asche legten und die Läden plünderten.

5 Seit fast zwei Dekaden setzt die britische Politik auf eine flächendeckende Videoüberwachung zur Verbrechensbekämpfung. Die Technik soll nicht nur terroristische Anschläge verhindern und Großveranstaltungen wie die Olympischen Spiele im kommenden Jahr sichern, sie ist dazu gedacht, ganz allgemein jede Art abweichenden, unsozialen Verhaltens aufzudecken. Videokameras als

10 neue Form sozialer Kontrolle.

Nils Zurawski, Jahrgang 1968, lehrt Soziologie an der Universität Hamburg. Seine Forschungsschwerpunkte sind Gewalt und Konfliktforschung sowie Informations- und Kommunikationstechnologien.

Millionen Pfund hat Großbritannien in die Technik gesteckt. Und die *Metropoli-*

15 *tan Police* von London ist stolz auf ihre Aufklärungsquoten – mehr als 1 000 Täter habe sie in diesem Jahr bereits identifiziert, verkündete sie im Mai. Nun, nach unzähligen Stunden gefilmter Krawalle, könnten es einige mehr werden. Momentan setzt die Polizei darauf, die Bilder der Kameras zu veröffentlichen und somit eine bewährte Methode bei der Verfolgung von mutmaßlichen Straf-

20 tätern massenhaft auszudehnen. Zusätzlich setzt sie eine für die Olympischen Spiele 2012 entwickelte Gesichtserkennungssoftware ein. Das Testfeld hätte nicht besser sein können.

Es scheint also, als ob die flächendeckende Videoüberwachung ihren Zweck erfüllt hat. Dabei hat sie in Wahrheit kläglich versagt – auch nach den Maßstäben

25 der Polizei. Denn weder konnten die Kameras auch nur einen der Aufstände verhindern, noch halfen sie der Polizei dabei, ihre Einsätze sinnvoll zu steuern.

Und auch eine umfassende Aufklärung dürfte schwierig werden: Die Fahndung wird zweifelsohne viele falsche Verdächtigungen hervorbringen, weil etliche der Bilder von schlechter Qualität sind, aus ungünstigen Winkeln aufgenommen

30 wurden oder schlicht zu falschen Schlussfolgerungen führen werden, wie der britisch-kanadische Überwachungsforscher David Murakami Wood zu be-

denken gibt. Obendrein sind bisherige Erfahrungen mit Gesichtserkennungsprogrammen nicht eben positiv ausgefallen.

Die Bürgerrechts-Organisation Big Brother Watch vermutet, dass allein zwi
35 schen 2007 und 2010 rund 300 Millionen britische Pfund für Kameras ausgegeben wurden. Davon hätte man, so die Rechnung, 4 500 Polizisten einstellen können – zweifellos eine bessere Maßnahme zur Vorbeugung als alle Videoüberwachungstechnik. Sicher, man darf Polizisten nicht mit Sozialarbeitern verwechseln, doch angesichts der Hilflosigkeit der britischen Polizei zu Beginn der
40 Krawalle wäre mehr Personal eine gute Investition gewesen.

Das fordert auch die Polizei selbst, tatsächlich aber steht sie vor massiven Kürzungen. Gut möglich, dass die Regierung Cameron nun genau die umgekehrten Schlüsse zieht – und die vielen Kamerabilder von den Krawallmachern als Beleg für den Erfolg des Systems heranzieht.

45 Die britische Kameraüberwachung nach diesen Aufständen aber als Erfolg zu verkaufen, ist zynisch, wenn man bedenkt, welchen Schaden Menschen, Nachbarschaften und die lokale Wirtschaft genommen haben. Ihnen allen hat die Videoüberwachung nicht geholfen. Beim nächsten Mal wird das nicht anders sein.

50 Deshalb darf die Diskussion über die Krawalle nicht in einer Forderung nach mehr Technik enden. Die Überwachungsgesellschaft, wie sie in Großbritannien seit Jahren Realität ist, kann solche Aufstände nicht verhindern. Sie ist schlicht nicht in der Lage dazu. Warum, so fragt Big Brother Watch, wurde mit viel Geld die Privatsphäre der Bürger jahrelang verletzt oder riskiert, wenn es eine
55 Sicherheit für sie dann doch nicht gibt? Die Frage ist berechtigt.

Im besten Fall können die Kamerabilder aus London, Manchester, Birmingham und anderen Städten nun dabei helfen, zu verstehen, was passiert ist: Möglicherweise nützen sie bei der Analyse, wie solche Krawalle entstehen, und wie man dagegen vorbeugt.

60 Die Unruhen in Großbritannien wären ein Anlass, um über die vielen Probleme der britischen Gesellschaft nachzudenken. Bürger und Politiker müssten sich fragen, was falsch läuft in ihrem Land, und welche Möglichkeiten der Vorbeugung und Sicherheit es jenseits des massiven Technikeinsatzes gibt. Leider aber muss man annehmen, dass die Politik auch dieses Mal wieder die falschen
65 Schlüsse ziehen wird. *(609 words)*

von Nils Zurawski, 13. 08. 2011; Quelle: Zeit Online;
http://www.zeit.de/politik/ausland/2011-08/london-krawalle-kameras/komplettansicht

I Mediation

(40 pts)

Du hast einen der begehrten Ferienjobs im British Council in Berlin bekommen. Zu deinen Aufgaben gehört es, eine Vortragsreihe über „Die britische Gesellschaft – gestern und heute" vorzubereiten. Einer der Referenten wird einen Vortrag über die Effizienz des britischen Überwachungssystems halten, worüber er bereits einen Artikel veröffentlicht hat.

Da der Referent den Vortrag auf Deutsch halten wird, jedoch ein Teil des Publikums englischsprachig und ohne Deutschkenntnisse ist, sollst du die wesentlichen Punkte des Artikels kurz schriftlich zusammenfassen, damit ein Handout verteilt werden kann.

Orientiere dich dabei an folgenden Fragen:

- Weshalb verfügt Großbritannien über so viele Überwachungskameras?
- Wie geht die Polizei mit Hilfe der Kameras vor?
- Wie schätzt der Autor die Effizienz vor dem Hintergrund der Krawalle von 2011 ein?
- Welche Schlüsse wird die Politik nach Meinung des Autors aus den Vorfällen ziehen?

II Conditional clauses

(10 pts)

Complete the following sentences with the correct forms of the verbs in brackets.

1. If the riots _____ (to deal with swiftly) by the authorities in London, they would not have spread north.

2. If you recognise individuals in the photographs released by the police, _____ (to contact) the Major Investigation Team.

3. Unless the quality of the pictures taken by the CCTV cameras is good enough, the suspects _____ (not to convict) by a court.

4. If Paul had not accidentally been there during the riots, he _____ (not to be) worried now.

5. What would you do if you _____
   (to accuse) of participating in the riots?

6. Many crimes could have been prevented if the money spent on
   CCTV technology _____ (to spend)
   on more police staff.

7. If the police officers watching the camera footage _____
   (to patrol) the streets, the citizens would feel safer.

8. The police _____ (to have to be)
   better prepared and trained if they are to improve their response
   to similar scenes of violence in the future.

9. If the number of police officers is further reduced, the public
   _____ (not to feel) safer – despite
   all the CCTV cameras.

10. Would the government pay attention to the social issues fuelling
    the riots if there _____ (not to be)
    any violence?

III Comment   (30 pts)

Choose <u>one</u> of the following subjects and write about 200 words.

1. CCTV surveillance, preventive data retention by the government,
   biometric passports. What is more important: protecting individual privacy or protecting public safety? Discuss.

2. "We will all know what everybody is doing all the time. Social
   networking is the end of privacy." Discuss.

Solution

Großbritanniens Überwachungssystem ist gescheitert

I Mediation

For almost twenty years, the British government has been relying on an extensive camera system to fight against crimes. It is not only supposed to deter terrorist attacks and make major events safer, but it is also a means of social control since it is used to detect anti-social behaviour.

With regard to the riots, the London Metropolitan Police are about to release pictures taken by the cameras so that the general public can help identify the alleged offenders. In addition to this, they use new facial recognition software.

So, on the surface, the ubiquitous monitoring appears to be efficient. But in fact it has failed completely because the cameras could not prevent a single incident from occurring during the riots, nor could they help the police be more effective in deploying their officers. In addition, the CCTV footage will not be sufficient to identify reliably those involved in the riots because of the poor quality of the pictures or because they were taken from a bad angle or might simply lead to wrong conclusions. And so far, experiences with facial recognition technology have not been positive either.

Nevertheless, there is the possibility that, in view of the extensive camera footage of the rioters, Cameron's government will jump to the conclusion that this is evidence of the success of the surveillance system. However, this point of view is cynical because people, neighbourhoods and the local economy all suffered damage which could not be prevented by the CCTV cameras.

The government has to recognise that despite ubiquitous monitoring such riots cannot be prevented. At best, the pictures taken might help to analyse the situation afterwards. But the riots should give us pause to consider the many problems British society has to face. Citizens and politicians should ask themselves whether there are other possible ways to make their lives safer besides this technology.

II Conditional clauses

1. If the riots **had been swiftly dealt with** by the authorities in London, they would not have spread north.

2. If you recognise individuals in the photographs released by the police, **contact** the Major Investigation Team.

3. Unless the quality of the pictures taken by the CCTV cameras is good enough, the suspects **will not be convicted** by a court.

4. If Paul had not accidentally been there during the riots, he **would not be** worried now.

5. What would you do if you **were accused** of participating in the riots?

6. Many crimes could have been prevented if the money spent on CCTV technology **had been spent** on more police staff.

7. If the police officers watching the camera footage **patrolled** the streets, the citizens would feel safer.

8. The police **will have to be** better prepared and trained if they are to improve their response to similar scenes of violence in the future.

9. If the number of police officers is further reduced, the public **will not feel** safer – despite all the CCTV cameras.

10. Would the government pay attention to the social issues fuelling the riots if there **had not been** any violence?

III Comment

1. In the 20th century the governments of many Western countries have introduced different methods of keeping the public under surveillance.
   CCTV cameras have been installed in public places to deter crime and grant public security. But this kind of constant surveillance limits people's freedom of expression and assembly.
   The biometric passport, which includes an electronic chip that stores fingerprints and an image of the holder's face, is supposed to reduce the risk of forgery and theft. But these data are also stored in a central database – and who can ensure that they are not passed on to a third party or otherwise misused?
   And the government's plans for preventive data retention have met with a lot of criticism recently because, under this new law, every citizen is treated like a potential suspect.

All these methods are said to be necessary in order to protect public safety. However, they also interfere unduly with individual privacy and nobody can control to whom their data are transmitted. The government should balance the efficiency of the methods with the level of intrusion into the individual's privacy – and recognise that it is not necessary to offend every citizen's personal rights in order to (try to) detect those who are about to engage in criminal activity.

2. Name, e-mail address, sex, date of birth – these pieces of information are required if Internet users want to sign up for a social networking sites. And when creating a profile more information will be given away because sharing private thoughts and daily happenings with friends has become a habit for many people. No problem if only friends can see it – but what if everyone could see it?

On the one hand, people using social networking sites do not know whether the site actually treats their data confidentially. Despite ways to keep certain information private, users do not really know who will see their personal details or read their comments. Again and again, social networking sites hit the headlines because of privacy issues, e. g. for storing personal data which users had actually deleted.

On the other hand, it is the users' responsibility what information they provide. They should be aware that inappropriate pictures can be seen by potential employers and that posting too much personal information is an open invitation to cyberbullies and stalkers.

In the end, it is all about being cautious when using social networking sites because the Internet never forgets: once the information has been copied by other people and saved on their hard drives, you really have lost control over it.

Notenschlüssel:

1	2	3	4	5	6
80–70	69–60	59–50	49–40	39–26	25–0

60 minutes

Mr Rosenblum's List

In 1937, Jack and Sadie Rosenblum leave Germany and emigrate to England be-
cause the situation is becoming more and more dangerous for Jews. Jack is deter-
mined to become a perfect English gentleman. He observes the English and keeps a
list of what he thinks is "typically English". After starting a very successful carpet
factory, he and his wife move to the countryside, where Jack wants to build his own
golf course because, as a Jew, he is not allowed to join an English one.

"May I show you into the rose garden? Sir William and Lady Waegbert will join
you shortly, Mr Rosenblum, Mrs Rosenblum."
They followed the servant into the formal garden at the front of the manor[1]. Jack
still found the English manner of speaking most peculiar. They so rarely made
5 absolute statements or asked you to do something but instead continually spoke
in rhetorical questions – "would you?" "may I?" – when what they truly meant
was park here, wait here. They liked to give you the illusion of choice, when really there was none.
"Will you be quite comfortable here, sir? And may I bring you a drink, sir?"
10 "Yes. Thank you. A whisky."
"With soda or ice?"
Jack paused, wondering which was the correct answer. Which would give him
away as a phoney[2] and a foreigner? "A dash of soda, please," he said, trying to
sound casual.
15 Symonds gave a tiny bow and Jack relaxed – he had chosen wisely. […]
"And for the lady?"
Now it was Sadie's turn to look stricken[3], she shifted uncomfortably from foot
to foot, heels sinking awkwardly into the grass. Nice, middle-class Jewish ladies
didn't drink. […]
20 "A gin and tonic, with a slice of lemon if you've got it," said Jack firmly.
Sadie opened her mouth to speak and then she shut it again meekly[4], smoothing
an imaginary crease[5] in her dress. She was still clutching the flowers.
"May I take these, madam?" asked Symonds.
Sadie hesitated. "They're for Lady Waegbert."
25 "The man doesn't think they're for him," said Jack irritably.
She allowed him to take them from her, watching as he vanished into the house.
They were left standing on a lawn, neatly clipped […]. She wondered whether it
was usual to be left hanging about in the garden, waiting for one's host.

191

In fact it was not. Lady Waegbert liked to greet her guests personally – however
30 unwelcome. She could not see why her husband had invited such ludicrous
people to her house – just because people were odd it was no guarantee of their
being entertaining. And now, they had arrived so outrageously early that no one
was ready to receive them.

"Surely *everybody* knows that seven o'clock means seven thirty," she com-
35 plained bitterly to her husband.

"Darling, they are foreign, *Germans*. They are always punctual."

"They are not punctual. They are early," she said, as if it were one of the worst
crimes in society. […]

The Rosenblums […] were oblivious to their violation of the social niceties. Nor
40 did Jack realise that they had been invited solely for entertainment value. The
other ten guests had all been asked to stay for dinner, and Jack was intended to
provide the pre-dinner cabaret. Sir William was not a cruel man but he enjoyed
the bizarre or ridiculous, and he had heard the strange tales about the Jew of Bulbarrow[6], who was trying to build a golf course in forty days and forty nights
45 with only a shovel. This was too good an opportunity to forgo[7] […].

The fact [that Jack] wore a suit […] for what was merely drinks was also highly
entertaining. A gentleman wears a jacket and tie for drinks and a suit only for
dinner. Sir William, however, was the model of perfect breeding and, as he
shook their hands with real warmth and profuse[8] apologies at his own lateness,
50 Jack and Sadie suspected nothing.

The remainder of the guests arrived punctually late at seven thirty. […]

The men drew around Sir William eager to meet the promised Jew, like a crowd
gathering for a circus act. […]

"So, do tell us about this golf course, then. The only reason we've come to this
55 ghastly pile[9] at all is to hear about it," said Mr Horare.

Jack looked worried – he recognised this to be an instance of English wit but did
not like it and hoped Sir William had not taken offence. The baronet, however,
remained unperturbed and smiled encouragingly.

"Well, the course will be the greatest in the whole South-West. It is the most im-
60 portant labour of my life," Jack declared.

He looked at the expectant faces and took another sip of whisky. […]

Across the lawn […] Lady Waegbert tried to get a better look at Jack's shoes
which, as she rightly suspected, were made of suede[10]. This was really too much
for Lady Waegbert, who viewed suede as a symptom of moral degeneracy[11].
65 […] Sadie's skirt length, cut at the knee instead of mid-calf in the New Look,
merely revealed her to be a woman without style […].

It was nearly eight thirty and time for dinner. These people should have gone by now. The middle-classes or Jews – they were all the same to her – never knew
70 when to leave. It was most unpleasant. If they did not go soon, she would be forced to ask them to stay, and that would be frightful. [...]   *(816 words)*

from Natasha Solomons, "Mr Rosenblum's List", Sceptre 2010, pp. 110–113, 116.

Annotations
1 manor – a large house in the countryside with land
2 phoney – sb. who is not genuine; fake
3 stricken – afraid
4 meekly – gently; unwilling to argue
5 crease – a line made by pressing, folding or wrinkling
6 Bulbarrow – Bulbarrow Hill is a well-known hill in Dorset
7 to forgo – not to profit from
8 profuse – many; in a large amount
9 ghastly pile – here: an awful looking large building
10 suede – type of leather that is slightly rough on one side
11 degeneracy – the act of sinking to a lower level

I   Working with the text   (50 pts)

Read all the tasks first. Then complete them in the given order. Use
your own words as far as appropriate.

1. Characterise Jack.

2. Jack and Sadie are not familiar with the conventions of high society. Explain what they do not know regarding social etiquette/
   'social niceties' (l. 39) in England.

3. Illustrate what Sir William and Lady Waegbert think of the
   Rosenblums.

II   Modal auxiliaries   (20 pts)

You are staying in Great Britain with your family. Sometimes, there
are situations where it is difficult to know how to behave correctly.

Use different auxiliaries and their substitutes respectively with the
words in brackets to formulate your reactions to the following situations.

1. Your friend is late for your date and says, "The stupid bus did not
   stop for me at the bus stop, so I had to walk all the way!"
   (→ give advice: next time – put out your hand)

   _____

   _____

2. Your brother tells you about a conversation with an Englishman
   he met at the pub: "When I mentioned the euro, he got really
   annoyed."
   *(→ express a criticism and mention another possibility: not –
   talk about that; weather)*

   _____

   _____

3. Your parents are planning a trip from London to Bristol by train.
   The weather forecast is for snow, which is quite unusual for the
   south of Great Britain.
   *(→ make a prediction and a suggestion: train – be cancelled;
   better – next weekend)*

   _____

   _____

4. You are sitting in a hot and stuffy train compartment and want to open a window.
   (→ *ask politely for permission: open the window*)

   _____

   _____

5. When in a café in Bristol, your father wants to light a cigarette.
   (→ *remind him of the rules and explain the alternative: not – inside; go outside*)

   _____

   _____

6. Your sister tells you that on the escalator to the Tube, she stood on the left-hand side and there were some very unfriendly people who snapped at her to move on.
   (→ *give advice: next time – stand – right-hand side*)

   _____

   _____

7. Your mother doesn't speak to English people because she is afraid to make mistakes.
   (→ *tell her it is not necessary: not – worry*)

   _____

   _____

III Mediation   (30 pts)

Before you left for London with your family, you bought a guide book in which there is a page about "Umgangsformen in Großbritannien", which seemed quite useful. When Peter, one of your new English friends, sees the book, he wants to know what it says.

Write a dialogue in English in which you summarise the most important "Benimmregeln" for him. Ask him whether he agrees with them or not. What does he reply? Use your knowledge about the English to complete his answers.

Umgangsformen in Großbritannien

Im Allgemeinen sind die Briten eher entspannt. Auch wenn sie ruhig und zurückhaltend erscheinen, heißt das nicht, dass sie unfreundlich sind. Ein gewisses Maß an Höflichkeit und gute Manieren werden erwartet, auch von Fremden.

 **Begrüßung:** Bei der ersten Begegnung wahren die Briten eher eine gewisse Distanz. Umarmungen und Begrüßungsküsse sind selten, der Händedruck ist nur beim ersten Treffen üblich. Am besten wartet man ab, bis einem die Hand gereicht wird. Ansonsten reicht ein kurzes „Hello" oder eine der anderen Begrüßungsfloskeln, wie beispielsweise „How do you do?" (Achtung: Die Antwort hierauf ist „Thank you. How do you do?").

 **Einladungen:** Wenn man von einem Briten nach Hause eingeladen wird, kann man gerne eine Kleinigkeit mitbringen, z. B. Blumen oder Pralinen. Wenn es etwas Landestypisches gibt, können Ausländer natürlich auch das als kleines Geschenk mitbringen und dem Gastgeber erklären, was es ist.

 **Schlange stehen:** Wenn Leute in einer Schlange warten, muss man sich am Ende anstellen und warten, bis man an der Reihe ist. Briten werden sehr ärgerlich, wenn man sich vorzudrängeln versucht.

 **Höflichkeit:** Höflichkeit wird in Großbritannien großgeschrieben. „Please" und „thank you" sind sehr wichtige Worte und werden häufiger verwendet als in den meisten anderen Ländern. Wenn man etwas möchte sollte man immer „please", und wenn man etwas erhalten hat, immer „thank you" verwenden. Wenn sich jemand bedankt, gehört es zum guten Ton, „you're welcome" zu entgegnen.

 **Tabu:** Zu den Themen, die man als Ausländer zunächst vermeiden sollte, bis man seinen Gesprächspartner besser kennt, gehören Nordirland, Religion, die Monarchie und die königliche Familie, die EU und der Euro … Und bitte beachten Sie: Sowohl Schotten als auch Waliser sind Briten, aber sie sind keine Engländer! Mit dem Ausdruck „the British" machen Sie nichts verkehrt.

Solution

Mr Rosenblum's List

I   Working with the text

1. Jack is an intelligent person who closely notices the cultural differences between the English and the Germans. He is, for example, aware of the fact that the English use a lot of courtesy phrases (cf. ll. 4–8). His main aim is not to give himself away as a foreigner, so he is very concerned about doing the right thing all the time (for example when choosing a drink, cf. l. 12) and even patronises his wife in order to avoid her making the wrong decision (cf. l. 20).

   He works tenaciously on his own golf course, which will be "the most important labour of [his] life" (ll. 59/60). For the others, this is quite a ludicrous undertaking but Jack takes it very seriously.

   Although he is quite smart, he is rather naïve at the same time. His view is limited to what he thinks he knows about the typical Englishman. He is so proud to be a baronet's guest that he does not realise that he is actually being made to look like a fool (cf. ll. 39/40).

2. Jack and Sadie do not feel comfortable when waiting for their hosts. Obviously, they have never received such an invitation before. That is why Sadie, for example, does not want to give the flowers for Lady Waegbert to the servant (cf. ll. 22–26). They are kept waiting because they did not know that an invitation for seven o'clock requires the guests to arrive about half an hour later (cf. l. 34).

   While Jack is not correctly dressed for the occasion because he put on a suit (cf. ll. 47/48), Sadie's dress is not of the latest fashion (cf. l. 65). In addition to this, Jack and Sadie are not aware that an invitation for drinks implies that the guests leave before dinner (cf. l. 41).

3. Sir William considers Jack, "the Jew of Bulbarrow" (ll. 43/44), quite a ridiculous person because he wants to build a golf course all on his own (cf. ll. 44/45). He has invited Jack over to his house in order to show his other guests what a fool Jack is and takes pleasure in making fun of Jack.

   The fact that the Rosenblums arrive too early for the invitation is attributed to them being Germans (cf. l. 36).

   Whereas Sir William greets the Rosenblums with genuine friendliness (cf. l. 49), Lady Waegbert judges them by their appearance (cf. ll. 62–66) and is eager for them to leave because otherwise she would be forced to ask them to stay for dinner (cf. ll. 70/71). She blames them for not knowing how to behave because they are "middle-class or Jews" (l. 69).

II Modal auxiliaries

*✎ **Hinweis:** Hier sollst du auf eine kurz beschriebene Situation angemessen reagieren und dabei modale Hilfsverben bzw., falls notwendig, ihre Ersatzformen verwenden. Es ist jeweils vorgegeben, ob du z. B. einen Rat geben oder Kritik äußern sollst. Die in Klammern angegebenen Wörter sollen dir auch dabei helfen. Natürlich kannst du sie noch ergänzen.*

✎ Sollten dir die modalen Hilfsverben und ihre Ersatzformen Schwierigkeiten bereiten, lies im Grammatikteil am Anfang dieses Buches nach.

1. Next time, you should / You have to put out your hand so that the driver knows that you want to be picked up.

2. You ought not to have talked about the euro or the EU with somebody you don't actually know. Next time, you could talk about the weather, that's always a safe topic.

3. If it really snows, the train will probably be cancelled. So you had better postpone your trip to next weekend.

4. May I open the window? / Would you mind me opening the window?

5. You are not allowed / You must not smoke inside the café. You should go outside to smoke.

6. Well, next time you should / ought to stand on the right-hand side, so that people can pass you on the left-hand side.

7. You needn't worry – the British will try to understand you.

III Mediation

*✎ **Hinweis:** Der deutsche Text dient als Vorlage für einen Dialog, in dem ein Gesprächspartner den Inhalt im Wesentlichen zusammenfassen soll. Durch die Dialogform hast du die Möglichkeit, den zweiten Gesprächspartner entsprechend reagieren zu lassen und evtl. sogar zusätzliche Information (z. B. über die aktuellen Begrüßungsrituale) einfließen zu lassen.*

PETER: So, what does it say about etiquette in Great Britain?

YOU: Well, they say here that when you meet somebody for the first time, British people do not usually hug or kiss, and they shake hands only when meeting for the first time. So it's best for a foreigner to wait till the other person offers their hand. Normally, a short "hello" or "how do you do?" is enough.

PETER: Yeah, that's true. We don't shake hands as often as you do in Germany, but it's getting increasingly frequent around here. And the girls sometimes kiss each other on the cheeks, like the French do.

YOU: Look here. It says that when you are invited to someone's home, you can take a little something with you, such as flowers or chocolates or something typical of your country.

PETER: Well, you do that here in Germany, too, don't you? It's always nice, although there is no rule about taking something.

YOU: The next paragraph is about queuing, your favourite pastime. It says that when there is a queue, you have to join the end of it and wait your turn. British people will turn on "queue jumpers".

PETER: How true! We British take waiting in line very seriously.

YOU: There is something else that you take extremely seriously: politeness. It says here that you should use "please" and "thank you" whenever possible, and not forget to answer "you're welcome".

PETER: Your guide book is really quite good, isn't it?

YOU: Is this also true: as a foreigner, you are supposed to avoid topics such as Northern Ireland, religion, the monarchy and the Royal Family, the EU and the euro?

PETER: Well, unless you know about the other person's attitude, they're not really very good topics if you want a relaxed conversation …

YOU: And, last but not least – and I know that by the way – it says that you mustn't call Scottish or Welsh people English.

Notenschlüssel:

1	2	3	4	5	6
100–88	87–75	74–64	61–50	49–33	32–0

60 minutes

Nightmare in gray

He awoke feeling wonderful, with the sun bright and warm upon him and spring in the air. He had dozed off – for less than half-an-hour, he knew, because the angle of shadows from the beneficent sun had changed but slightly while he slept – sitting upright upon the park bench; only his head had nodded then fallen for-
5 ward.

The park was beautiful with the green of spring, softer green than summer's, the day was magnificent, and he was young and in love. Wondrously in love, dizzily in love. And happily in love; only last night, Saturday night, he had proposed to Susan, and she had accepted him, more or less. That is, she had not given him a
10 definite yes but she had invited him this afternoon to meet her family and had said that she hoped he would love them and that they would love him – as she did. If that wasn't tantamount to[1] an acceptance, what was? They'd fallen in love at first sight, almost, which was why he had yet to meet her family.

Sweet Susan, of the soft brown hair, with the cute little nose that was almost
15 pug[2], of the faint, tender freckles and the big, soft brown eyes.

She was the most wonderful thing that had ever happened to him, that could ever happen to anyone.

Well, it was midafternoon now and that was when Susan had asked him to call. He stood up from the bench and, since he found his muscles a bit cramped from
20 the nap, yawned luxuriously. Then he started to walk the few blocks from the park where he had been killing time to the house he'd taken her home to last night, a short walk through the bright sunshine, the spring day.

He climbed the steps and knocked on the door. It opened and for a second he thought Susan herself had answered it, but the girl only looked like Susan. Her
25 sister, probably; she'd mentioned having a sister only a year older than she.

He bowed and introduced himself, asked for Susan. He thought the girl looked at him strangely for a moment. Then she said, "Come in, please. She's not here at the moment, but if you'll wait in the parlour[3] there –"

He waited in the parlour there. How odd of her to have gone out. Even briefly.
30 Then he heard the voice, the voice of the girl who had let him in, talking in the hallway outside and, in understandable curiosity, stood up and went to the hall-way door to listen. She seemed to be talking into a telephone.

"Harry – please come home right away, and bring the doctor with you. Yes, it's Grandpa … No, not another heart attack. Like the time before when he had am-

35 nesia[4] and thought that Grandma was still – No, not senile dementia, Harry, just amnesia, but worse this time. Fifty years off – his memory is way back before he even married Grandma …"

Suddenly old, aged fifty years in fifty seconds, he wept silently as he leaned against the door … *(512 words)*

NIGHTMARE IN GRAY by Fredric Brown. Copyright © 1961 by Fredric Brown, copyright © 1989 by the Estate. Originally appeared in NIGHTMARES AND GEEZENSTACKS. Reprinted by permission of the Estate and its agent.

Annotations
1   tantamount to – virtually the same as
2   pug nose – a short nose with an upturned tip
3   parlour – a room for receiving visitors
4   amnesia – a partial or total loss of memory

I   Working with the text   (30 pts)

1.   Summarise this short story in your own words.

2.   There are some instances of foreshadowing in the story. Explain them.

3.   Comment on the title.

II   Language and form   (30 pts)

1.   Which characteristics of a short story can you identify in the text above? Explain them briefly.

2.   Identify two literary or stylistic devices (besides foreshadowing) and describe the use the author makes of them.

III   Picture analysis   (20 pts)

Choose <u>one</u> of the following pictures and answer the questions below.

1.   What do you see in the picture? Describe the picture in as much detail as possible.

2.   What relationship do the people have to each other? Why are they in this place? What did they do before and what will they do afterwards? Use your imagination.

Picture A

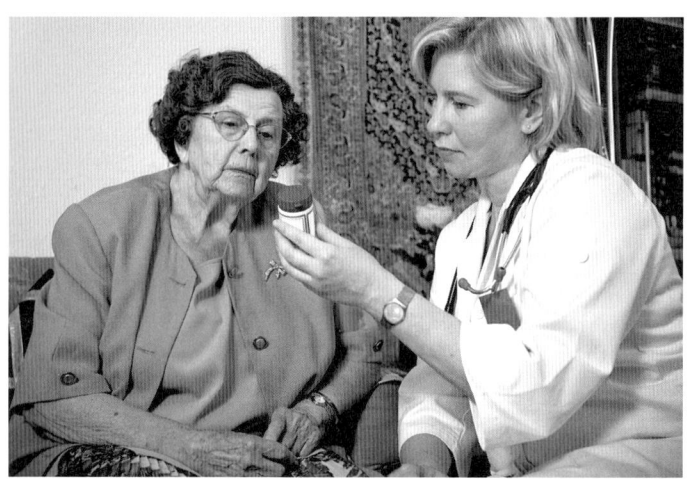

Picture B

Solution

Nightmare in gray

I   Working with the text

1. The short story "Nightmare in gray" by Fredric Brown, deals with the problems of old age and dementia. The protagonist of the story wakes up in a park after a nap on a bench. He remembers proposing to Susan, the girl he is in love with, the night before. She invited him to meet her family. So he heads for the house she lives in.

    When he knocks, a girl opens the door. He thinks that she is Susan's sister because she looks like her. The girl asks him in and while he waits for Susan, he overhears the girl talking on the phone. She explains to somebody that her grandfather is there and is suffering from amnesia because he does not even remember marrying her grandmother. That is when the protagonist becomes aware of the fact that he is actually old and the girl not the sister of his wife-to-be but his granddaughter.

2. The surprise ending is alluded to in different places in the story. For a young man (cf. l. 7) it is rather unusual to take a nap in a park, but the main character "dozed off" (l. 2) there in the afternoon. When he stands up from the bench, his muscles are tense and he has to stretch before going (cf. ll. 19/20). This is also a hint that he is not a young man anymore. When he knocks at Susan's door, he realises that "the girl looked at him strangely for a moment" (ll. 26/27), so she knows something the reader does not yet know. The girl's behaviour is also bizarre because she leaves the room (cf. ll. 30/31), something she would not normally do when having a guest. The protagonist also finds it "odd" (l. 29) that his wife-to-be is not at home, although she had told him to come.

3. The title "Nightmare in gray" refers to the fact that the protagonist "aged fifty years in fifty seconds" (l. 38); that, all of a sudden, he realises that he is actually an old man – probably with grey hair – who cannot remember large parts of his life. Growing old, especially when suffering from amnesia, is a real nightmare for him, only it is not a dream but a frightening reality.

II   Language and form

1. The short story begins in medias res, showing a supposedly young man somewhere in a park in spring. There are only two characters: the protagonist and the girl that opens the door. The plot of the story is simple and shows a decisive moment in life: a young man who is to meet the family of

his future wife. The story ends rather abruptly and surprisingly for the reader and leaves one with a vivid sensation of sympathy and wanting to know how the story goes on for the protagonist.

2. The author uses the words "in love" (ll. 7/8) several times in a row to describe the protagonist's emotional state. He even intensifies this **repetition** three times, saying: "Wondrously in love, dizzily in love […] happily in love" (ll. 7/8). That way, the author underlines how important this feeling is for the protagonist. It seems like nothing else matters to him at that moment. When describing the wife-to-be, the author uses a **hyperbole** to reinforce the fact that the protagonist is incredibly happy: "She was the most wonderful thing that had ever happened to him, that could ever happen to anyone" (ll. 16/17).

III Picture analysis

Hinweis: Hier sollst du eines der Bilder auswählen und zunächst genau beschreiben, was du siehst. Als zweiten Teil der Aufgabe sollst du dir ausdenken, in welcher Beziehung die Personen zueinander stehen, warum sie sich in dieser Situation befinden und was sie vorher getan haben bzw. nachher tun werden. Hier gibt es keine richtigen oder falschen Antworten. Es kommt darauf an, dass du dir eine plausible Situation überlegst und deine Ideen entsprechend präzise formulierst. Die beiden folgenden Antworten sind nur Beispiele, natürlich kannst du ganz andere Assoziationen haben.

Picture A

1. In the picture, there are two elderly people, a man and a woman. The man has got short, grey hair and is wearing a light-coloured pullover. The woman has got short, black hair and is wearing a light-coloured T-shirt or light pullover and a white cardigan over her shoulders. They seem to be outside or in front of a window since there is something that looks like part of a fence in the background. The woman is holding a mobile phone so that both of them can listen to what is being said on the phone.

2. The two people are probably married. They are phoning their son, who is abroad for a gap year. They want to find out whether he is fine and getting along without any problems. Before phoning him they went for a walk and talked about him and their other children. After the call, they will have dinner together.

1. In the picture, there are two people, an elderly woman and a young woman. The elderly woman has got short, dark, curly hair. She is wearing glasses, a T-shirt and a short blazer with a brooch attached on one side. On her left wrist, she is wearing a watch. She is looking attentively at the little pill bottle that the younger woman is holding. The younger woman has got medium-length blonde hair and is wearing a watch on her left wrist. She is obviously a doctor or a nurse because she is wearing a lab coat and a stethoscope around her neck. She is looking intently at the pill bottle and seems to be reading the text on the label.

2. The younger woman is the older woman's doctor, who received a call because the older woman was suffering from heart problems, so she came over to the elderly woman's flat. Before the visit, the doctor made some more calls to other patients and the elderly woman had a friend over for tea. Afterwards, the doctor will go back to her office and the elderly woman will watch TV.

Notenschlüssel:

1	2	3	4	5	6
80–70	69–60	59–50	49–40	39–26	25–0

60 minutes

I   Listening comprehension: Population tops 7 billion* (Track 8)

1. Multiple choice   (1 pt.)
   Which sentence describes the overall topic of the text best?

   ☐ The birthday of the seven billionth person on earth.

   ☐ The challenges that population growth implies.

   ☐ The problems of developing countries with regard to population growth.

2. True or false   (8 pts)
   Decide whether the following statements are true or false. If a
   statement is false, correct it.   true   false

   a) The United Nations think that the world's popu-   ☐   ☐
   lation has reached seven billion people.

   _____

   _____

   b) The seven billionth person was born on October   ☐   ☐
   31.

   _____

   _____

   c) We depend on population growth politically and   ☐   ☐
   economically .

   _____

   _____

   d) The population has grown from two to seven   ☐   ☐
   billion people in a very short time.

   _____

   _____

* *Podcast from 2010*

3. Answer the following questions in note form.   (6 pts)

a) How many of the world's continents are inhabited?

_____

b) Which is the most populated continent?

_____

c) Which are the two main problems that population growth implies?

_____

_____

d) Where does Koeber see the main problem for the United States?

_____

4. Add the correct information.   (8 pts)

In rather _____ countries, such as the United States, the population level is _____. But these countries use a _____ amount of resources and produce a lot of _____ and

_____.

Lesser developed countries, on the other hand, have _____

_____ populations. They, too, consume their resources rapidly, but with the aim to _____ and _____ on a daily basis.

5. Explain in your own words why "a larger population globally makes the issue of food more complicated".   (7 pts)

II Visual analysis and mediation   (30 pts)

Answer the following questions with the help of the diagram below. The diagram is in German, but your answers should be in English in complete sentences.

1. How did the world population develop between 1950 and 2010? Speculate on the reasons for this development.

2. How will the situation continue to develop in the future?

3. What can you say about the curve progression?

4. How is the population distributed across the different continents?

5. Will this distribution stay the same in 2100? Interpret the development.

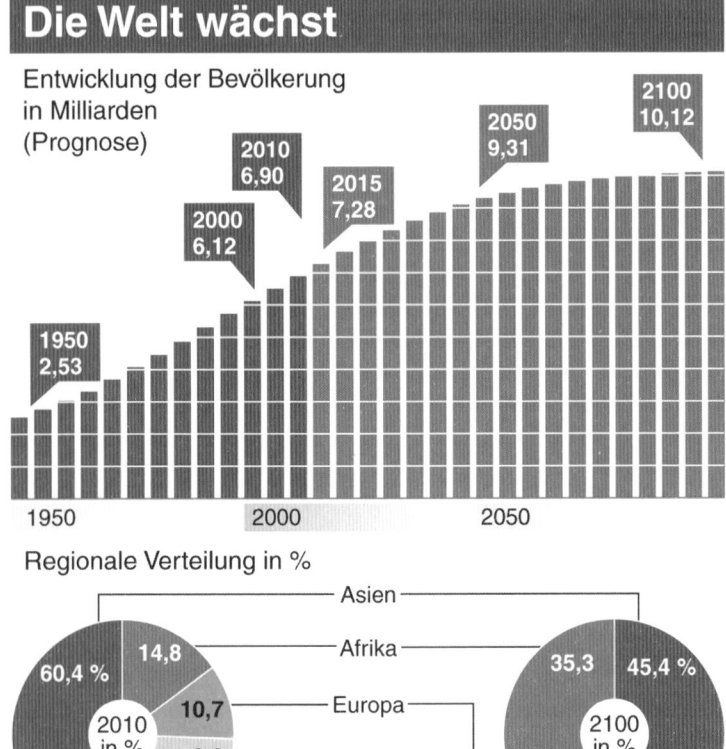

Die Welt wächst

Entwicklung der Bevölkerung
in Milliarden
(Prognose)

2100
10,12

2050
9,31

2010
6,90

2015
7,28

2000
6,12

1950
2,53

1950   2000   2050

Regionale Verteilung in %

Asien

Afrika

Europa

Lateinamerika/
Karibik

Nordamerika

Ozeanien

60,4 %   14,8   10,7   8,6   5,0   0,5
2010
in %

35,3   45,4 %   6,7   6,8   5,2   0,7
2100
in %

rundungsbedingte Differenz

dpa•14620 Quelle: UN, Stiftung Weltbevölkerung (Projektion: mittlere Variante)

picture-alliance/ dpa-Grafik

III Tenses and the passive voice   (20 pts)

Put the verbs in parentheses into the correct tense. Use the passive voice where necessary.

Since nobody _____ (to know) precisely when the world's population _____ _____ (to pass) the seven billion mark, the United Nations _____ (to select) October 31, 2010, to symbolically mark the day. In many countries around the globe, newborn babies _____ (to choose) to symbolise the seven billionth human. Celebrations of their birthday _____ (to mark) this population milestone and _____ (to aim) at drawing attention to global population growth.

The first of these babies _____ (to be born) in the Philippines, one of the world's poorest countries. The baby girl _____ (to give) a lot of gifts, such as a birthday cake, a college scholarship grant and financial aid for her parents, who _____ (to plan) to open a small business for a long time. Despite all this, it _____ (to seem) that most of these symbolically chosen children _____ (to live) on the wrong side of the poverty line. Experts and demographers _____ (to predict) that a dark future _____ (to lie) ahead of them – and ahead of the whole world – if the challenges that _____ (to come) with a population growth of that scale _____ (not to address) efficiently.

The estimates regarding the development of population growth, however, _____ (to vary) widely because they _____ (to depend) on a lot of factors, such as life expectancy, access to birth control and infant mortality rates. At the moment, total population _____ (still, to climb), but the rate of global growth _____ (to reach) its all-time high in the 1960s at about 2 percent. Since then, it _____ _____ (continuously, to decline).

Solution

Population tops 7 billion (Tapescript)

Hinweis: *Diese Hörverstehensaufgabe beschäftigt sich damit, dass die Weltbevölkerung 2010 die 7-Milliarden-Grenze überschritten hat. Der vorliegende Text
erläutert die Schwierigkeiten, die dadurch auf uns zukommen. Dass diese nicht
immer leicht zu lösen sein werden, beschreibt der Moderator als eine „Catch-
22". Das ist ein Ausdruck, der eine Situation bezeichnet, bei der die Lösung eines
Teilproblems andere Probleme nach sich zieht.*

You're listening to the podcast edition of the Wichita State University audio news-
line. Learn more about WSU on the Web at wichita.edu.

PRESENTER: Without a lot of fanfare, the world population topped 7 billion people
about Oct. 31, according to United Nations' estimates. The actual date may be
fuzzy, but there's no mistaking the challenges facing the world, according to
Wichita State University sociologist Charles Koeber.

KOEBER: If you listen to politicians and economists, we are dependent on growth for
our economy and to sustain our population, so growth is not necessarily a bad
thing. However, when you look at the world consisting of a finite amount of resources, it does raise some important questions about how much we can grow.

PRESENTER: Koeber says it's hard because most of us can't comprehend how large
7 billion is.

KOEBER: "So the population being 7 billion, that's a very large number. However,
it's been a very large number for a very long time, and I don't think people can
really comprehend how large it actually is.

Seven billion is kind of like a birthday. When you're 5 or 10 years old, it's a big
deal. That's when we had maybe 1 or 2 billion. But when you get into your 40s
and 50s, it's just another birthday, and that's what 7 billion is.

PRESENTER: The world's population is unevenly distributed, with six of the world's
seven continents being permanently inhabited on a large scale. Asia is the most
populated of earth's continents, with more than 4 billion inhabitants accounting
for more than 60 percent of the world's population. Koeber says the growing
world population presents some challenges.

KOEBER: Environmental sustainability and energy are key issues. When we look
down the road, we have to be able to replace our sources of energy and our natural
environmental resources at a rate that's equal to that which we're consuming
them.

PRESENTER: In the United States, the issue isn't so much the size of the population
as the amount of resources being consumed, as Koeber explains.

KOEBER: Population alone is not the only issue. You have to look at the level of af-
fluence. So, for example, the United States, a very affluent country with a lower

211

level of population, is using a disproportionate amount of resources and contributing to a disproportionate amount of waste and pollution.

PRESENTER: In lesser developed countries, the challenge is survival and meeting needs.

KOEBER: In lesser developed countries that have large populations, the problem is more related to survival and need. So they may be using up their resources at incredibly fast rates just for the population to survive and stay alive on a daily basis.

PRESENTER: Koeber says as the world population grows, a major concern is whether there will be enough food to go around.

KOEBER: A larger population globally makes the issue of food more complicated. And while technology has kept up in being able to produce enough food, the problem is distribution, and you have all sorts of factors including civil strife, politics, economic policy that interfere with the distribution of food in different areas.

PRESENTER: Paul Ehrlich of Stanford University, famous for his book "The Population Bomb," said people will have trouble feeding themselves as climate change worsens. But it's a Catch-22, he said, because we need to expand agriculture, but as it's practiced today it is also one of the biggest emitters of greenhouse gases.

Thanks for listening. Until next time, this is Joe Kleinsasser for Wichita State University.

I Listening comprehension

1. Which sentence describes the overall topic of the text best?

   ☐ The birthday of the seven billionth person on earth.

   ☒ The challenges that population growth implies.

   ☐ The problems of developing countries with regard to population growth.

		true	false
2. a)	The United Nations think that the world's population has reached seven billion people.	☒	☐
b)	The seven billionth person was born on October 31. **The actual date when the population reached seven billion is not known.**	☐	☒
c)	We depend on population growth politically and economically.	☒	☐
d)	The population has grown from two to seven billion people in a very short time. **The population has been very large for a very long time.**	☐	☒

3. a) **six/6 (out of seven/7)**

   b) **Asia**

   c) **environmental sustainability and energy**

   d) **in the amount of resources being consumed**

4. In rather **affluent/wealthy** countries, such as the United States, the population level is **low**. But these countries use a **disproportionate** amount of resources and produce a lot of **waste** and **pollution**.
   Lesser developed countries, on the other hand, have **large(r)** populations. They, too, consume their resources rapidly, but with the aim to **survive** and **stay alive** on a daily basis.

5. According to Koeber, the question is whether a larger population will have enough food supplies. The problem is not the food production, since the technology is up to it, but whether the food can be distributed to where it is needed. Distribution can be affected by various factors, such as economic policies, for example. In addition to that, climate change also plays a role: it affects different areas negatively; therefore agriculture has to be expanded. At the same time agriculture is one of the biggest emitters of greenhouse gases.

II Visual analysis and mediation

1. Between 1950 and 2010, the world population increased from 2.53 billion to 6.9 billion, which means an increase of about 4.4 billion people within 60 years.
   This rapid population growth is due to the fact that death rates could be reduced because of improved public health, increased food production, better food distribution and medical technology (e. g. vaccines and antibiotics). In addition to that, education levels increased and so living standards improved in many parts of the world.

2. The world population is projected to exceed 9.3 billion by 2050. Estimates say that it will top 10 billion in 2100.

3. Whereas the global population increased relatively rapidly from 1950 onwards and almost tripled by 2015 according to the prognosis, the growth rate is expected to slow down and almost stagnate in the last few years covered by the diagram.

4. In 2010, Asia is by far the most populated region. More than 60 % of the world population live here. In second place is Africa with 14.8 % of the

world population. The remaining quarter of the estimated 6.9 billion people reside in Europe (10.7 %), Latin America and the Caribbean (8.6 %), North America (5 %) and Oceania (0.5 %).

5. In 2100, Asia will still be the most inhabited continent, but it will only have 45.4 % of the world's population, which means a decline of 15 %. Africa will more than double its percentage, with 35.3 % of the world's population living on this continent. Europe, on the other hand, will lose 4 percentage points and Latin America 2 percentage points. The population in North America and Oceania will increase negligibly.

It seems that the world population growth will be concentrated in the world's poorer countries, which have a higher average fertility rate than the more affluent countries, where the numbers will only slightly increase or even decline.

III Tenses and the passive voice

Since nobody **knew** precisely when the world's population **would pass** the seven billion mark, the United Nations **selected** October 31, 2010, to symbolically mark the day. In many countries around the globe, newborn babies **were chosen** to symbolise the seven billionth human. Celebrations of their birthday **marked** this population milestone and **aimed** at drawing attention to global population growth.

The first of these babies **was born** in the Philippines, one of the world's poorest countries. The baby girl **was given** a lot of gifts, such as a birthday cake, a college scholarship grant and financial aid for her parents, who **had been planning** to open a small business for a long time. Despite all this, it **seems** that most of these symbolically chosen children **will live** on the wrong side of the poverty line. Experts and demographers **predict** that a dark future **will lie** ahead of them – and ahead of the whole world – if the challenges that **come** with a population growth of that scale **are not addressed** efficiently.

The estimates regarding the development of population growth, however, **vary** widely because they **depend** on a lot of factors, such as life expectancy, access to birth control and infant mortality rates. At the moment, total population **is still climbing**, but the rate of global growth **reached** its all-time high in the 1960s at about 2 percent. Since then, it **has continuously declined**.

Notenschlüssel:

1	2	3	4	5	6
80–70	69–60	59–50	49–40	39–26	25–0

> ## Klassenarbeit 14
> ### Schwerpunkte: *Listening and reading comprehension, writing*

60 minutes

I **Listening comprehension: Freedom Rides** (Track 9)

Listen to the text and complete the tasks. The following information may help you to understand the context:

Jim Crow laws

The Jim Crow laws are state and local laws in the USA enacted primarily, but not exclusively in southern and border states between 1877 and the mid-1960s. Under these laws, African Americans were relegated to the status of second-class citizens by way of racial segregation in all public facilities, e.g. in public schools, restaurants, public transportation or drinking fountains.

KKK

KKK is the abbreviation for Ku Klux Klan, a far-right, extremist organisation in the United States convinced of the superiority of the white race.

1. Finish the sentences by ticking the correct answers.
   Several answers may be correct.   (12 pts)

   a) The Freedom Rides in the American South …

   ☐ took place at the beginning of the 1950s.

   ☐ were organised by Black and white protesters.

   ☐ wanted to test laws against the discrimination of Black Americans.

   ☐ were stopped by the Jim Crow laws.

   b) The press coverage of these rides …

   ☐ showed photos of violent incidents.

   ☐ was in favour of the non-violent protesters.

   ☐ raised awareness for the issue all over the world.

   ☐ was important for the bus companies.

c) Indigenous people in Australia …

☐ supported the protesters in the USA.

☐ were also discriminated against.

☐ had a right to state assistance.

☐ did not have legal rights for their own children.

2. Decide whether the following statements are true or false.
Correct the false statements.

| | true | false | (14 pts) |

a) In the 1950s and early 1960s, campaigns against ☐ ☐
the discrimination of Aboriginal people spread
around Australia.

_____

_____

b) Discrimination was particularly bad in the larger ☐ ☐
cities.

_____

_____

c) After watching the protests in the USA, students ☐ ☐
in Sydney organised the Australian Freedom
Rides.

_____

_____

d) Australian students protested against the attempt ☐ ☐
to block the American Civil Rights Act.

_____

_____

e) Some people considered it hypocritical to protest ☐ ☐
against racial discrimination in other countries as
long as Aboriginal people were still discriminated
against in Australia.

_____

_____

3. Complete the summary of Charles Perkin's life.   (24 pts)

Charles Perkins was born _____ near
Alice Springs. Like many mixed-raced children, he was taken
away from _____ and sent to _____

_____.

He had a talent for _____ and played as a
professional. But when he was offered the chance to play for
_____, he did not accept. Instead he re-
turned to Australia because he wanted to devote himself to the
case of _____ at home.

As a student at the University of _____ he was
head of the SAFA group, short for "_____

_____".

Charles Perkins was the first Aboriginal person _____

_____ and _____

_____.

II Working with a poem   (20 pts)

Analyse the experiences of Black people according to the following
song:

Big Bill Broonzy: Black, Brown and White (1951)

1 This little song that I'm singin' about,
   People, you all know that it's true,
   If you're black and gotta work for livin',
   Now, this is what they will say to you,
5 They says: If you was white,
   You's alright,
   If you was brown,
   Stick around,
   But if you's black, oh, brother,
10 Get back, get back, get back.

   I was in a place one night,
   They was all havin' fun,
   They was all buyin' beer and wine,
   But they would not sell me none.

15 They said: If you was white,
   You's alright,
   If you was brown,
   You could stick around,
   But as you's black, hmm, hmm, brother,
20 Get back, get back, get back.

   I went to an employment office,
   I got a number, I got in line,
   They called everybody's number,
   But they never did call mine.
25 They said: If you was white,
   You's alright,
   If you was brown,
   You could stick around,
   But as you's black, hmm, hmm, brother,
30 Get back, get back, get back.

   Me and a man was workin' side by side,
   Now, this is what it meant:
   They was payin' him a dollar an hour,
   And they was payin' me fifty cent.
35 They said: If you was white,
   You'd be alright,
   If you was brown,
   You could stick around,
   But as you's black, oh, brother,
40 Get back, get back, get back.

   I helped win sweet victories,
   With my plow and hoe,
   Now, I want you to tell me, brother,
   What you gonna do 'bout the old Jim Crow?
45 Now, if you is white,
   You's alright,
   If you's brown,
   Stick around,
   But if you's black,
50 Hmm, hmm, brother,
   Get back, get back, get back.

Big Bill Broonzy: Black, Brown and White. Album: Black, Brown and White
© *Evidence Music 1995*

III Composition

(20 pts)

On August 28, 1963, Martin Luther King, Jr. delivered his most famous speech, in which he said: "I have a dream that one day this nation will rise up and live out the true meaning of its creed [i. e. a religious belief]: 'We hold these truths to be self-evident: that all men are created equal.'"

Analyse to what extent Dr. King's dream has been realised today, more than 50 years later.

Solution

Freedom Rides (Tapescript)

Welcome to Stuff you missed in History Class, from howstuffworks.com.

SARAH DOWDEY: Hello and welcome to the podcast. I'm Sarah Dowdey.

DEBLINA CHAKRABORTY: And I'm Deblina Chakraborty.

SARAH DOWDEY: ... and we are still talking about the Freedom Rides. So we've been talking about them now for a little while, but we've been talking about the Freedom Rides that took place in the American South in 1961. And, just in case you missed those earlier episodes, it was about groups of protesters – Black and white, male and female – from all over the country who rode buses through Virginia, the Carolinas, Tennessee, Georgia and, most notably, through Alabama and Mississippi, to test laws that were already in place, but were large ... largely overridden by local Jim Crow tradition.

DEBLINA: Yep, and one thing we kept emphasising throughout those episodes was the press coverage of the rides, especially the photos. People across the U.S. saw these images of beaten up students, a bus on fire, and violent mobs going up against non-violent protesters. But the thing is that people around the world saw those images too, not just in the U.S., even all the way in Australia, where they really struck a chord. Australian society was also segregated along racial lines, since the Aboriginal and the Torres Strait Islander Australians were essentially second-class citizens, underserved in housing and health care, ineligible for federal benefits, and often without legal rights for their own children.

SARAH: And I think that's the part that most people know about: Aboriginal people, that loss of their children, the stolen generation. But in the 1950s and the early 60s, campaigns for Aboriginal rights were starting to gain ground in Australia, but the fact remained that many Australians in the larger cities just weren't really aware of how bad discrimination and how bad conditions were in the smaller interior towns and on the reservations, so a publicity-fueled event like an Australian version of the Freedom Rides would be possibly just the thing to kind of shake them up, wake them up a little bit.

DEBLINA: Right, but we can't act as though there was just this neat direct jump through from the students in Sydney watching students in Nashville and immediately going out and staging their own Freedom Rides. Instead, and kind of ironically, it was a later U.S. civil rights event that jumpstarted the Australian Freedom Rides, and that was the 1964 Civil Rights Act. So, while the Act was being debated in Congress, students in Sydney showed their disapproval of the attempts to block the bill by dressing up as KKK members and protesting outside of the U.S. embassy.

SARAH: This obviously caused quite a ruckus, as you could imagine. There were arrests, there were international headlines and, unsurprisingly, there was some backlash too. A Mrs. R. Shodde, for instance, wrote into the Sydney Morning Herald to point out, kind of the obvious here: until Aborigines had the same rights as white Australians, it was a bit hypocritical to protest racial discrimination in other countries. So, the students really took that point to heart and they decided to form a group and try to deal with this, try to learn more about racism in their own country. So, these students at the University of Sydney formed a new group to focus on Australian issues and they called it the "Student Action for Aborigines" – SAFA for short – and it was headed up by Charles Perkins. And Perkins is a pretty well-known figure for most Australians, I think, but, I'm not sure, I hadn't heard of him before and I'm not sure how [DEBLINA: "Yeah, me neither."] well-known he is outside of Australia. He eventually became the first Aborigine to earn a university degree, and that's probably what he's most famous for. He was also the first to head up a government department. But he had been born on a reservation near Alice Springs and, like a lot of mixed-raced children, he had been removed from his parents and raised in an Anglican boys' home. But, unlike a lot of the other children, who had fewer opportunities, he was really, really good at soccer and he had gotten to go play pro in England and finally even turned down an offer with Manchester United. I think even those of us who don't know much about soccer know about Manchester United.

He turned down an offer with them to return back to Australia and play as captain for one of the local clubs. And there was a two-part reason for that: I mean, one, it's a good soccer opportunity, but the other is that living abroad had made him think more about devoting himself to Aboriginal rights at home. He wanted to … he wanted to be at home and he wanted to make a difference.

DEBLINA: Yeah, enough to give up a huge opportunity to play for one of the biggest leagues in the world. So, with Perkins at the head of the SAFA, the group started planning something big, and they decided to follow the model of the U.S. Freedom Riders. […]

http://podcasts.howstuffworks.com/hsw/podcasts/symhc/2011-09-26-symhc-freedom-riders-part-3.mp3?_kip_ipx=911831441-1321952111

I   Listening comprehension

1. a)   The Freedom Rides in the American South …

   ☐   took place at the beginning of the 1950s.

   ☒   were organised by Black and white protesters.

   ☒   wanted to test laws against the discrimination of Black Americans.

   ☐   were stopped by the Jim Crow laws.

   b)   The press coverage of these rides …

   ☒   showed photos of violent incidents.

   ☐   was in favour of the non-violent protesters.

   ☒   raised awareness of the issue all over the world.

   ☐   was important for the bus companies.

   c)   Indigenous people in Australia …

   ☐   supported the protesters in the USA.

   ☒   were also discriminated against.

   ☐   had a right to state assistance.

   ☒   did not have legal rights for their own children.

		true	false
2. a)	In the 1950s and early 1960s, campaigns against the discrimination of Aboriginal people spread around Australia.	☒	☐
b)	Discrimination was particularly bad in **smaller towns and on reservations**.	☐	☒
c)	**The Australian Freedom Rides did not start immediately after the American ones.**	☐	☒
d)	Australian students protested against the attempt to block the American Civil Rights Act.	☒	☐
e)	Some people considered it hypocritical to protest against racial discrimination in other countries as long as Aboriginal people were still discriminated against in Australia.	☒	☐

3.   Charles Perkins was born **on a reservation** near Alice Springs. Like many mixed-raced children, he was taken away from **his parents** and sent to **an Anglican boys' home.**
He had a talent for **soccer** and played as a professional. But when he was offered the chance to play for **Manchester United,** he did not accept. In-

stead he returned to Australia because he wanted to devote himself to the case of **Aboriginal people/Aboriginal rights** at home.

As a student at the University of **Sydney** he was head of the SAFA group, short for "**Student Action for Aborigines**".

Charles Perkins was the first Aboriginal person **to earn a university degree** and **to head (up) a government department**.

II Working with a poem

The song "Black, Brown and White" by Big Bill Broonzy is about the reality of segregation as Black people had to face it. The first-person narrator represents the Black people living in a white society. Right at the beginning, he states that the situation of the Black people he is going to describe is well-known to everybody (cf. l. 2).

He points out the inequity in treatment and pay: For a Black person it is hardly possible to lead a decent life and earn a living because white people or people of mixed race are preferred by employers (cf. ll. 5–8). A Black person is not even invited to a job interview (cf. l. 24) and if he has got a job, he is paid less than a white or mixed-race person (cf. ll. 33/34). In a bar or a restaurant, a Black person is not served, while white and brown people are having a good time (cf. ll. 12–14).

And although Black Americans work hard to support their society and country (cf. ll. 41/42), they do not receive any kind of acceptance, but suffer from racial segregation in all areas of life.

As repeated in the chorus, Black people have to "get back", i. e. they have to stay away from the others. White people are accepted everywhere and people of mixed race are allowed to stay, although this does not really imply approval.

III Composition

When Dr Martin Luther King delivered this famous speech in 1963, African-Americans were not at all free and equal to whites. Black people were treated as second-class citizens in every area of life. Since then, considerable progress has been made in terms of racial equality and social justice, although the problem of prejudice certainly continues to exist.

Life for African-Americans has certainly improved. Racial segregation in education, public transport and other public places has been dismantled. They have become professors and teachers, mayors, senators and managers. Barack Obama is living proof that African Americans can achieve higher political and economic status, but he did not become the first Black president without having to face hatred and disdain on the way.

Martin Luther King wanted every person to have equal opportunities – educationally, economically, culturally and politically – irrespective of the colour of their skin or ethnicity. However, even today, Black and white people are far from being equal when it comes to average income, home ownership, education, life expectancy, the incarceration rate and drug use. African Americans are still targets of hate crimes or police violence. In all these respects, Dr King's dream remains unfulfilled. Further progress will have to be made in order to achieve his aims.

Notenschlüssel:

1	2	3	4	5	6
90–79	78–67	66–56	55–45	44–30	29–0

15–20 minutes

I **Presentation (1 minute per candidate)**
Introduce yourself and talk about your favourite leisure activities.

II **Comment (3–4 minutes)**
Work together with your partner.

Talk about **immigration:**
What effect can ethnic minority groups have on a country?
Talk about both positive aspects and possible problems.

III **Role play (4–5 minutes)**
Read through the role cards quietly. Together with your partner choose **one** of the following situations. Decide who is A and who is B and act out the dialogue.

a)
Candidate A

You have been invited to a friend's party on Friday. But today (Thursday), you had a terrible row with some of your friends from your class. You don't feel like going to the party. You tell B that you won't be going.

Candidate B

It is your party. You have heard about the row and you know that it was based on misunderstandings. You try to convince A to come to the party.

b)
Candidate A

You have had problems with your parents and at school for a while. Today there was another dispute with your parents. So you have decided to run away. You tell your friend about your reasons and your plans.

IV Describing a picture (5 minutes)

Take turns to describe your picture in as much detail as possible.
Then compare your pictures and talk about the message together.

A

B

Solution

Hinweis: Die Bewertung der Sprachkompetenz der Prüflinge in einer mündlichen Prüfung erfolgt im Allgemeinen nach folgenden Kriterien: Aussprache und Intonation, Flüssigkeit, Wortschatz, grammatische Korrektheit und Inhalt. Je nach Aufgabe werden diese Kriterien unterschiedlich gewichtet. Bei dem Teil der Prüfung, der zusammen mit einem Partner oder einer Partnerin zu bearbeiten ist, wird außerdem die Interaktion in die Bewertung einbezogen. Vor einer mündlichen Prüfung wird deine Lehrkraft erklären, welche Kriterien angelegt werden und wie sie gewichtet sind.

I Presentation

Hinweis: Viele mündliche Prüfungen beginnen mit einer persönlichen Frage, damit der Prüfling sich in seine Rolle einfinden kann. Auf diese Fragen kannst du dich vorbereiten, indem du schon vorab überlegst, wie du dich selbst vorstellen kannst und was dir wichtig ist.

Sample solution: talking about yourself and your favourite leisure activities

My name is Anna-Lena Meyer and I live here in Neustadt bei Coburg. I'm 16 years old and I'm in year 10 at the Arnold-Gymnasium. My favourite subjects are English, history and physical education. I really enjoy taking part in all the extra-curricular activities that are offered at our school. I've been the chief editor of our school magazine since last year and I like writing articles about things that are interesting to me and my schoolmates. I'm also a member of the team of pupils who are responsible for first aid at school. So I usually spend quite a lot of time at school during the week. When I'm not at school and not busy doing my homework, I like swimming and running. At the moment, I am training to run a half-marathon in summer, which takes quite a bit of my spare time. Apart from that, I love reading books and watching films either at the cinema or at home with my family and friends.

II Comment

Hinweis: Auch diese Aufgabe kannst du im Vorfeld der Prüfung vorbereiten. Lege dir bestimmte nützliche Füllwörter und Gesprächsfloskeln bereit, z. B.:
– *Well, I don't think so …*
– *I'm sorry, but I don't agree at all.*
– *I think you're right up to a point.*
– *What I want to say is …*
– *What do you think about …*
– *As far as I'm concerned …*
– *Do you mind if I interrupt?*

PARTNER A: This morning, there were some more official statistics on the number of immigrants in the newspaper. Have you seen them?

PARTNER B: No, I haven't. Was there anything special?

PARTNER A: Well, in fact, the article was about the effects that ethnic minority groups can have on a country. Have you ever thought about that?

PARTNER B: Well, I think that in people's minds, immigrants, that is to say ethnic minorities, are connected to lots of problems society is facing nowadays. Many people hold prejudices against people of a different skin colour or a different religious or cultural background – especially after what happened in New York and London.

PARTNER A: Yeah, I know what you mean. After 9/11, every Muslim was viewed with suspicion as if every single one were a terrorist. Those prejudices are terrible – you cannot tar everyone with the same brush.

PARTNER B: I totally agree. But lots of people are of the opinion that immigrants come to our country in order to benefit from the money our welfare state grants them. Many think that they take away our jobs and are therefore the reason why the unemployment rate is so high. But, let's be honest, often they just do the jobs that our own people don't want to do.

PARTNER A: Well, you know, I can't by any stretch of the imagination understand these people. First of all, they should know some facts about immigration and those affected. In fact, I believe that people from a different ethnic background can enrich the culture of the host country enormously. Just think about the different kinds of food. I love eating out at Chinese restaurants and imagine that there were no doner kebabs! Unthinkable!

PARTNER B: Yes, you're right. Immigrants can make a great contribution towards the culture of a country as far as food or literature are concerned. But to a certain degree, they also have to adapt to the country where they want to live.

PARTNER A: That's a good point. That's often discussed by politicians these days. Well, I believe that the immigrants should at least learn to speak the country's language as this is essential for their children to be able to grow up in a different culture.

PARTNER B: Yes, I agree.

III Role play

🖊 **Hinweis:** *Hier sollen du und dein*e Prüfungspartner*in ein spontanes Ge-*
🖊 *spräch führen, ohne dass ihr vorher gemeinsam überlegen könnt, welchen*
🖊 *Verlauf das Gespräch genau nimmt. Am besten beginnt ihr das Gespräch je*
🖊 *nach vorgegebener Situation mit ein oder zwei einleitenden Floskeln (z. B.*
🖊 *"Nice to see you. How are you?"), um dann auf das Thema zu sprechen zu*
🖊 *kommen. Diese Phrasen kannst du dir schon vor der Prüfung zurechtlegen.*
🖊 *Höre dann genau zu, was dein*e Gesprächspartner*in sagt und gehe auf das,*
🖊 *was er oder sie sagt, ein. Sollte das Gespräch ins Stocken kommen oder dein*e*
🖊 *Partner*in sprachliche oder inhaltliche Probleme haben, versuche ihm oder*
🖊 *ihr zu helfen, indem du beispielsweise Rückfragen stellst (z. B. "So, if I under-*
🖊 *stand you correctly …?; "Do you think that …?") oder einen Einwand*
🖊 *vorbringst (z. B. "May I interrupt you for a moment?"; "I'm sorry but I don't*
🖊 *agree at all."). Achte außerdem darauf, dass das Gespräch auf irgendeine*
🖊 *Weise einen Abschluss findet und nicht einfach abrupt zu Ende ist.*

a) PARTNER A: Hey, Sarah, have you got a second? I'd like to talk to you.

PARTNER B: Of course, Jessica, what's the matter?

PARTNER A: Well, I just wanted to tell you that I don't feel like celebrating with all those idiots and that I won't be coming to your party tomorrow.

PARTNER B: Oh, don't be silly. Of course you will. Why shouldn't you? We've both been looking forward to it for ages.

PARTNER A: Yes, I know. But I've just had an argument with Janette and the others.

PARTNER B: What was it about?

PARTNER A: Oh, someone told me that Janette had said that I would only take part in the sports competition because then I wouldn't have to go to school and that I wouldn't have the slightest chance of winning because I'm so unsporty.

PARTNER B: That's the reason why you don't want to come? Well, calm down. Janette isn't coming to the party tomorrow because she'll be out of town. So, no problem there. But who told you what she was supposed to have said?

PARTNER A: Laura heard her talking about me and some others in the changing cabin after the PE lesson. And when I talked to Janette about what she'd said she just pretended not to know what I was going on about. Instead, she said that she'd never even said anything about me. As if I wasn't worth being talked about at all …

PARTNER B: Now, don't exaggerate. You know that Laura isn't exactly trustworthy. What about me talking to both of them and clearing up the situation? Then you won't have to worry about it anymore and you can enjoy the party tomorrow night. I'm sure that either Laura understood something completely wrong or she made it up because she's jealous.

PARTNER A: Okay, so tell me when you've talked to them. Actually, it's your party … and I don't have to talk to the others if I don't want to …

PARTNER B: Yes, you're right. But I'll make sure everything will be okay by tomorrow night, okay?

PARTNER A: Yes, okay. Thank you!

b) PARTNER A: Hey, Lena, have you got a minute to talk?

PARTNER B: Yes, sure! What's the problem? You look terrible. What has happened?

PARTNER A: Oh, it's just my parents again. You know, when they saw the maths test yesterday, we had a terrible row.

PARTNER B: I'm so sorry to hear that.

PARTNER A: It's always the same. They want me to do better at school. They always tell me to work more for maths and physics. And when I tell them that this is the best I can do, they're disappointed. They don't see that I'm good at art and English.

PARTNER B: Yes, and you're excellent at PE … But I know what you mean. For them those subjects aren't important.

PARTNER A: Exactly. And the teachers tell me that I'm no good at sciences either. That doesn't really help me.

PARTNER B: Well, don't take that too seriously. You know what kind of a person "Mr. Mathematics" is. He can just be really nasty.

PARTNER A: Anyway. I've packed my backpack and taken all the money out of my account and my savings box. Today I'm not going home after school. I've decided to run away.

PARTNER B: You have what?

PARTNER A: You heard right. The worst thing is that I don't even know whether they will realise that I'm gone. They only keep telling me to tidy up my room and to be home by 10. So for them, it'll be a relief when I'm gone.

PARTNER B: Oh, no, that's not true and you know it. Running away is not a solution to your problems. Have you ever talked to your parents about how you feel?

PARTNER A: Of course I have. But those conversations always end up in an argument about me not being like they want me to be. So I'll go and stay with a friend for a while.

PARTNER B: But that won't make the situation any easier for you. You're not old enough yet, so your parents are still in charge. And to be honest, parents are often like that. You have to find another way to talk to them.

Have you ever thought of seeing our guidance counsellor? She might be able to mediate so that you and your parents can have a calm conversation and talk things over.

PARTNER A: You're always so sensible … Well …, okay, I'll try that. But I'm not unpacking my bag yet …

IV Describing a picture

Hinweis: Bei dieser Aufgabe bekommen dein Mitprüfling und du unterschied-liche Bilder, die ein gemeinsames Thema haben. Während du dir überlegst, wie das Bild so genau wie möglich beschrieben werden kann, solltest du auch daran denken, welche Aussage dahinter stehen könnte. Folgende Fragen kön-nen dir bei der Bildbeschreibung helfen:

– What do the people in the picture look like (height, build, age, face, hair)?
– What are they wearing?
– What are they doing? Where are they?
– What relationship do they have to each other?
– What are they feeling and thinking? Why?

Da die Bilder gewisse Leerstellen lassen, kannst du hier natürlich plausible Vermutungen anstellen, z. B. was die Beziehung der Personen untereinander angeht.

A In the picture, there are five people: one teenager in the foreground and four young people in the background. The young man in the foreground is about sixteen years old and of medium height. He has got short, blonde, tousled hair and is wearing a dark T-shirt and glasses. In his arms, he is holding a bunch of folders and books. He seems to be very sad or disappointed, even close to tears.

The four people in the background are three young women and one young man about the same age as the boy in the foreground. The young man has his arm round one of the women. Obviously, the weather is fine because they are all wearing summer clothes: short-sleeved T-shirts and jeans. They are leaning against the wall of a public building, probably a school building. They are looking at the boy, who is not facing them, but has his back to them. One of the young women seems to be pointing at the boy.

Evidently, the four of them are having a good time – as opposed to the boy in the foreground.

B In the picture, there are three girls who are about sixteen years old. They have got long hair that they are wearing in a ponytail. The two girls on the left and right have dark hair and the one in the middle has light hair. The hair of the girl on the right is very curly and she looks as if she might be from a Latino background. They are wearing cheerleader dresses and hold-

231

ing pom-poms in their hands. The girls are putting their arms around each other's shoulders and the girls on the sides are resting their free hands on their waists. All three are very pretty and are smiling happily. Obviously they are friends and are having a good time before or after a match of their school team, which they cheer on. The picture is taken from a low-angle position and in the background you can see the sky. The weather is fine, so for the girls it's a good day.

The message:

PARTNER A: I think my picture shows a typical situation at school where there is a group of popular kids who stick together and other kids who are not accepted by them. Obviously, the teenagers in the background are talking about and making fun of the boy in the foreground, who is hurt by what they say. Perhaps they have called him a geek.

PARTNER B: Yes, I see what you mean. That might fit the message of my picture, as the cheerleaders of a school are often the most popular girls in a class or a school. Usually they are an exclusive group in which "normal" girls are not accepted.

PARTNER A: Well, I agree with you. At school there are often groups of popular kids and for those who do not belong to these groups it's really hard sometimes, especially when they are outsiders for one reason or another.

PARTNER B: Yes, a lot of kids are bullied by their classmates because they are different in some way. And some of them would do anything to belong to one of the popular groups.

15–20 minutes

I **One-minute-talk (1–2 minutes)**

Choose **one** of the following topics and give your opinion on it. Try to weigh your arguments.

a) Which is more important in **sports:** winning or taking part? Are you a good loser?

b) Would you like to work as a **volunteer in a developing country**? If so, in which country, and how could you contribute to that country's development?

II **Role play (4–5 minutes)**

Read your role card (one of you is A, one is B), think briefly about suitable arguments, then act out the dialogue with your partner.

Candidate A

You are 12 years old and you want to have a computer for your birthday. Your mother/father doesn't think that this is a good idea because of the dangers of the Internet. But you want to convince her/him that the Internet is a great opportunity to do a lot of useful things.

Put forward your arguments and try to find a compromise with your mother/father.

Candidate B

You are the mother/father of a 12-year-old daughter/son who wants to have a computer for her/his birthday. You don't think that this is a good idea as there are many dangers and negative aspects and you want to protect your child.

Put forward your arguments and try to find a compromise with your daughter/son.

III Talking about cartoons (5 minutes)

Take turns to describe your cartoon in as much detail as possible. Then compare your cartoons and talk about the message together.

A

B

"We're not intrusive – we keep a respectable distance."

Solution

I One-minute-talk

Hinweis: Bei dieser Aufgabe sollst du ein bestimmtes Thema möglichst struk- turiert von mehreren Seiten beleuchten. Es ist also wichtig, dass du nach einem einleitenden Satz zum Thema nicht nur positive Aspekte erwähnst, son- dern auch negative Gesichtspunkte zur Sprache bringst. Abschließend sollst du deine eigene Meinung äußern. Hierfür kannst du dir im Vorfeld der Prü- fung schon einige Phrasen zurechtlegen (z. B. "I hold the view that …"; "I am of the opinion that …"; "I am convinced that …"; "In my opinion, you have to take into account that …"; "I firmly believe that …").

a) At my school, there are a lot of different sports teams, such as the handball team, the tennis team and the football team. I'm a member of the swimming team and the volleyball team. We often take part in competitions or play friendly games against other schools. And sometimes, I wonder which is more important in sports: winning or taking part.

   Of course, we play for the sake of winning – as do most of athletes. The aim to win is absolutely crucial to success. Otherwise people wouldn't take their sports seriously. And when you take it seriously and work hard, winning is a source of valuable personal confidence. It's just a great feeling to be re- warded for all the time and effort that you put into practising.

   But I have to admit that I do not really care whether I or my team win or not as long as it's a good and fair game or competition. In this respect, I think sports can be a means to forming your character, as you have to learn to be patient and self-disciplined and to control your emotions.

   As for me, I think that I'm rather a good loser. Of course, it's more fun to win than to lose, but if it was a fair game and the best player won, I'm able to accept that fact. Being defeated and thus not satisfied with my perfor- mance is rather a reason to train harder in order to be better next time. In this regard, taking part is more important than winning because it makes me see my strengths and weaknesses.

b) The appeals for money on TV and in the newspapers, especially after some sort of natural disaster such as the earthquake in Haiti or the tsunami in Thailand, often make me realise that there are people around the world who are not as well-off as we are here in our industrialised country. And I have to say that I've often thought about working as a volunteer in a Third World country.

   Of course, I'm aware that this is not an easy job and it might often even be quite dangerous in some parts of the world because of ongoing wars or serious diseases. And it's certainly hard to experience the people's misery and poverty and suffering firsthand. That's the reason why I've always admired people who give up their lives in order to help others, like Karl-Heinz Böhm for example.

As far as I'm concerned, it's particularly important to give a good education to young people in developing countries so that they will someday be able to lead their country towards a better future. I could imagine going to an African country, such as Tanzania or Uganda, in order to help to build a school for children of poor families or even to teach them there. This could be my very small contribution towards a better future for these countries.

II Role play

Hinweis: Bei dieser Aufgabe weißt du, worauf das Gespräch hinauslaufen wird. Entscheidend sind also die Argumente, die du und dein*e Partner*in anführen können. Höre also gut zu, was dein*e Gesprächspartner*in sagt und versuche, darauf zu reagieren bzw. führe deine Argumente an geeigneter Stelle an. Denke daran, dass es hier eine klare Rollenvorgabe gibt (12-Jährige(r) und Elternteil), die es zu berücksichtigen gilt.

PARTNER A: Mum, I'd like to talk to you about my birthday present. You know that I'd like to have a computer for my birthday.

PARTNER B: Yes, Mike, I know. We've already talked about that and you know that I'm not really convinced that it's a good idea.

PARTNER A: But, Mum, nowadays it's absolutely essential to have access to the Internet. I often have to look something up for my homework and it's much quicker to do that on the computer than to search for the information in books that you only find in libraries. It's so easy with the Internet and you can find anything.

PARTNER B: That's true, but you can never be sure that the information is reliable because there is no quality control when it comes to information that is published on the World Wide Web.

PARTNER A: I know that I have to check if the information is valid. We've already been told by our teacher that there are unreliable sites on the web. For instance, we're not allowed to use Wikipedia as the only source.

PARTNER B: Well, that's good. But you know that the net can even be dangerous, especially if you give away personal information on websites or in chat rooms.

PARTNER A: But, Mum, I won't do that, I'm not stupid.

PARTNER B: I'm also afraid that you'll spend too much time in front of the computer. You won't only use it for school stuff, I'm sure.

PARTNER A: Of course not. To be honest, there's a computer game I'd like to have, too.

PARTNER B: So, playing computer games, sending e-mails, chatting, social networking, that takes a lot of time. Would you still have any time left to meet your real friends?

PARTNER A: Mum, you know me, I won't get addicted to all that stuff. I love meeting my friends in the park and playing football and tennis. So there'll always be enough time for those things.

PARTNER B: I know that you are really sensible. But I'm still not convinced that it's a good idea to have your own computer in your room …

PARTNER A: Oh, Mum …

PARTNER B: Perhaps we can reach a compromise. What about putting the computer on the spare desk in my office? Of course, you'll have your privacy, but you won't be all on your own if there's something you perhaps don't understand.

PARTNER A: Well, … okay. If you agree to it then.

PARTNER B: One more condition: If you want to join a social network or something where you have to give away any personal information, you will let Dad and me know so that we can check whether the site is trustworthy.

PARTNER A: Okay, I think that's fair … for a start.

III Talking about cartoons

Hinweis: Bevor du die Karikatur beschreibst, überlege dir, worum es geht, d. h. was das Thema ist. Beschreibe nur die Details, die für die Bedeutung der Karikatur wichtig sind, lasse unwichtige Details weg. Dann arbeite heraus, was die Karikatur illustriert und kritisiert und vergleiche die Aussage deiner Karikatur mit der des Partners.

A   In the cartoon, there are two women in short, black dresses. They are leaving a club which can be seen in the background. Apparently, the two women are celebrities because there is a bunch of paparazzi waiting for them and taking lots of pictures. The paparazzi are obviously pleased to take some snapshots of the women.

Whereas one of the women seems to be bothered by the presence of the photographers and calls them "bloody paparazzi", the other one reveals that it was she who phoned them to give away where they were. In fact, she is even upset that it took the paparazzi so long to come and take the pictures: "I know. It's at least forty minutes since I rang them!"

B In the cartoon, there are two people, a man and a woman, who are being followed by two paparazzi. The man and the woman seem to be celebrities
who have tried to disguise themselves. The woman is wearing a rather big
coat and both are wearing sunglasses in order not to be recognised. Nevertheless, the paparazzi have found them and are now taking pictures of them.
There is another man who is talking to the paparazzi. Evidently, he has criti-
cised the photographers for bothering the two celebrities. But one of the
paparazzi answers: "We are not intrusive – we keep a respectable distance."
In fact, there is some distance between the photographers and the celebrities, but ironically, the paparazzi use very long lenses that almost touch the
stars, so that they can photograph every tiny detail.

The message:

PARTNER A: My cartoon illustrates that it's sometimes the celebrities themselves
who call the photographers. They want to have pictures taken because that
keeps them in the press and it's part of their job that people talk about them
and are interested in them. It's often a way to promote their next film or show.

PARTNER B: I see your point. My cartoon on the other hand illustrates the fact
that sometimes the paparazzi do not really respect the celebrities' privacy but
are reckless when they want to take exclusive pictures that they can sell for a
lot of money. I think the most popular victim of these practices was Princess
Diana.

PARTNER A: Yes, that's true. But in Diana's case, that was really extreme.
Usually, the Royals try to get along well with the press. They regularly have a
deal with the journalists and have official appointments where pictures can be
taken. The rest of the time, the journalists are asked to respect their privacy.

PARTNER B: That's a good compromise. We mustn't forget that it's partly due to
the public's interest that the journalists are so eager to find out something interesting about the Royals or other celebrities, something everybody wants to
know about them. So for them it's necessary to hit the headlines with another
scandal or something else.